cushions
& quilts

I dedicate this book to my long-suffering husband, mum and whole family, including my staff at Cowslip Workshops who are also my quilting friends. Without all their support I would never have achieved my goal of stitching through life – a career hanging by a thread!

cushions
& quilts

JO COLWILL

QUILTING PROJECTS TO DECORATE YOUR HOME

David and Charles

www.stitchcraftcreate.co.uk

Contents

Welcome to Cowslip Country

Animals, the countryside and country life have inspired me since I was a young girl and provided endless ideas for sewing. This book offers some of those ideas in a collection of lovely cushions and quilts to enhance your home or to make as gifts for family and friends.

Inspiration is all around me on the farm where I live and work, including the glorious Cornish countryside, the day-to-day farming tasks and also my dogs and horses. I love the flowers in spring and enjoy capturing the lovely vibrant colours of buttercups with swallows flying low over them. Each season brings with it unique colours, skies and textures just waiting to be captured in fabric and thread.

When I married I changed from dressmaking to home-making and made my first quilt over thirty-five years ago. This led me into working in interior design, where I learned about colour and how it can affect your mood. My passion for colour, texture and fabrics, both new and old, grew from making home items into quilts and using every bit of spare fabric to make a comfortable home.

Patchwork and quilting, and especially the materials and techniques, have moved on since I began quilting. Today it is easier than ever to learn the basic techniques and then take them in your own direction, and I hope the projects here encourage you to do that. We all see fabrics and colours in different ways, which is one of the reasons why patchwork is so exciting and addictive.

In this book I describe my unique way of creating cushions and quilts. You can make the projects just as they are or modify the ideas to create your own individual style. Whether using vintage fabrics or brand new, you can escape into a wonderful world of fabric and stitches. I have designs stacked up in my head like planes waiting to land at an airport and always have a little project by my side ready for the odd five minutes of sewing.

For most of the projects, patchwork is combined with appliqué and hand embroidery and the sewing techniques are clearly described to help you achieve beautiful results. You can use needle-turn appliqué (my favourite) or fusible web, which is usually faster. Each project lists the materials needed, followed by step-by-step instructions with diagrams and photographs to help you make the project. The templates needed are included and general techniques and embroidery stitches are described at the end of the book.

Recording your life story in stitches is good for the soul and so relaxing as you become engrossed in a project. Don't worry if your stitching isn't flawless – practice makes perfect! So, have fun using the ideas in this book and like me, let one quilt or cushion lead to another, and another . . .

The Projects

Vintage Button Cushion

This cushion is great fun and really easy to make. It can be constructed from small squares using left-over bits of your favourite fabrics. You can even use labels from children's clothes, which will make treasured memories. Once you get the idea you can change the sizes of the squares to make a larger cushion, and then add borders in the same sequence.

The use of linen fabric creates a lovely country feel, with the easy quilting worked with a thick perle thread to create a bolder stitch. Small mother-of-pearl buttons add a decorative touch in the centre of some of the squares but you could use buttons rescued from old garments. Buttons are used again as a decorative fastening for the cushion.

Requirements

- Mixed fabrics, twenty-five 2½in (6.3cm) squares
- Linen or plain cotton for borders and backing, 30in (75cm) (width of fabric)
- Patterned fabric for lining/binding, 6½in (16.5cm) (width of fabric)
- Calico for lining, 22in (56cm) square
- Cotton wadding (batting), 22in (56cm) square
- Perle no.8 thread in ecru, for quilting
- Blending thread for piecing and a strong thread for sewing on buttons
- Mother-of-pearl buttons: five or six small ones for decorating the front and five large and five small for the cushion fastening
- Cushion pad, 18in (45.7cm) square (will be rolled in half)

Finished size: 19in x 13in (48.3cm x 33cm)

Instead of buying a square cushion pad and rolling it in half, you could use an oblong pad 18in x 12in (45.7cm x 30.5cm), if you can find one.

PREPARING FABRICS

1 Cut twenty-five 2½in (6.3cm) squares from your mixed fabrics. You could be very organized and cut five squares from five different fabrics or cut random squares as you go. Lay them out on your cutting board and shuffle them around until you feel happy with the design.

2 Cut one piece of linen 4in x 10½in (10.2cm x 26.7cm) for the left-hand border of the cushion. Cut one piece of linen 6in x 10½in (15.2cm x 26.7cm) for the right-hand border. Cut two pieces of linen each 2in x 19½in (5cm x 49.5cm) for the top and bottom borders.

3 Cut one piece of linen for the back of the cushion 13½in x 19½in (34.3cm x 49.5cm).

MAKING UP

1 Using a thread to blend with your fabric and ¼in (6mm) seams, sew the squares into rows as shown in Fig 1. Press the seams in the directions indicated in the diagram. This means that the pieced rows will 'lock' together and make the seams easy to match up when the rows are sewn together. Now sew the rows together and press the work.

2 Sew the 4in x 10½in (10.2cm x 26.7cm) linen to the left side of the pieced squares, and the 6in x 10½in (15.2cm x 26.7cm) piece to the right side, pressing the seams towards the squares. Now sew each 2in x 19½in (5cm x 49.5cm) piece of linen to the top and bottom and press towards the squares (Fig 2).

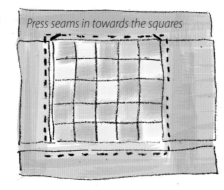

Press seams in towards the squares

Fig 2 *Adding the borders*

3 Layer the square of calico, wadding (batting) and patchwork to make a quilt sandwich (see General Techniques: Making a Quilt Sandwich). If you gently rub up the wadding there is no need to stick or tack (baste) the layers together for something this size. Using the ecru perle thread, quilt flower and heart motifs on the squares, using the templates supplied. Quilt crosses on some of the squares (see General Techniques: Quilting). Sew on small buttons to finish decorating the cushion front.

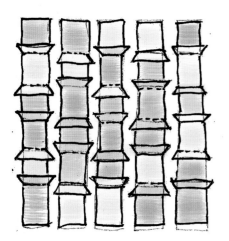

Alternate pressing helps the squares butt up together nicely and makes joining the rows easier

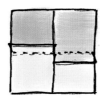

Fig 1 *Sew the squares into rows, pressing seams in alternate directions and then sew the rows together*

4 Take the piece of linen backing fabric and sew it to the cushion front along the top (Fig 3). Take the patterned fabric for the lining/binding and iron in ¼in (6mm) along the long edge. Fold over again and sew down to neaten the edge. Now place it face down on the right side of the cushion front and back and sew together with a ½in (1.3cm) seam (a larger seam than usual).

Fig 3 *Adding the back and the side lining*

5 Press the patterned fabric towards the backing to make a sharp line and then open out again. Fold the cushion right sides together, keeping the lining out. Using a seam allowance slightly larger than ¼in (6mm) seam, sew down the long side (making sure that the linings match front and back) and then continue sewing across the bottom (Fig 4). Clip corners and turn right side out.

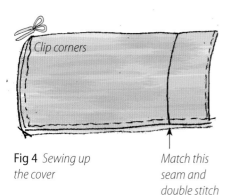

Fig 4 *Sewing up the cover*

Match this seam and double stitch

6 Push the lining inside the cushion to the pressed line, which will leave ½in (1.3cm) showing on the front (Fig 5). Topstitch very close to the seam.

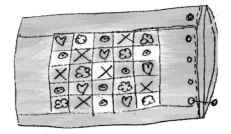

Fig 5 *Arranging the lining and then sewing on the buttons*

7 Insert the cushion pad, rolled in half. Lay five large buttons along the open edge and mark the positions. Sew on a large button, with a matching small one on the back, sewing through both buttons with a strong thread. This gives a very nice finish and avoids using buttonholes.

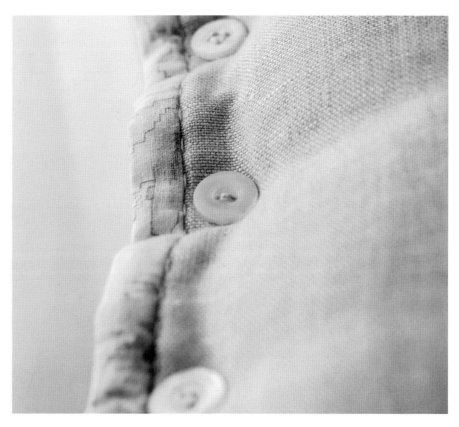

Faded Roses Cushion

We all have fabric stashes we'd like to keep under control and also need practice with machine or hand quilting and this pretty cushion will help you do both. Nice cushions for a summer evening party need not be too time consuming to make. There is nothing like sitting out on a warm evening with the scent of roses gently blowing in the air and a comfy cushion to nestle against. I have used the reverse of the ticked fabric on this cushion for a more subtle look, but you can choose what you want.

Polyester wadding (batting) was used on the cushion as it has more loft than cotton wadding and makes the quilting on the roses more pronounced.

Requirements
- Pale floral rose fabric for centre panel and ties, ½yd/m
- Black-and-white or blue-and-white striped pillow/herringbone ticking for piecing and cushion back, ½yd/m
- Polyester wadding (batting), 20in (50cm) square
- Calico lining fabric, 20in (50cm) square
- Small label (optional)
- Feather cushion pad 16in (40.6cm) square

Finished size: 16in (40.6cm) square

tip

When piecing together your cushion front you could try adding a small label for a stylish touch, sewing it into one of the seams. The writing on the selvedge of the fabric can also look very effective.

PREPARING FABRICS

1 For the cushion front, cut Piece A from floral rose fabric 8½in (21.6cm) square.
Cut Piece B from striped ticking 4½in x 8½in (11.4cm x 21.6cm).
Cut Piece C from striped ticking 12½in x 4½in (31.8cm x 11.4cm).
Cut Piece D from striped ticking 4½in x 12½in (11.4cm x 31.8cm).
Cut Piece E from striped ticking 16½in x 4½in (41.9cm x 11.4cm).

2 Cut wadding (batting) and calico for lining, each 17in (43.2cm) square.
Cut ticking for the back of the cushion 16½in (41.9cm) square.
Cut floral rose fabric 6½in x 33in (16.5cm x 83.8cm) for lining the buttonhole side.
Cut floral rose fabric for ties, two strips each 3½in x 22in (8.9cm x 55.9cm).

MAKING UP

1 Following Fig 1, and using ¼in (6mm) seams, join Piece A to Piece B and press towards Piece B. Add Piece C, then D and then E, always pressing towards the outside.

2 Make a quilt sandwich of the cushion front, wadding (batting) and calico. Tack (baste) around the outside edge by machine if you have a walking foot, using stitch length 5, or hand tack. If you use the machine without a walking foot the presser foot will push the fabric out of shape.

3 Either hand quilt or machine quilt with the darning foot using free quilting (often called free-motion or freehand quilting). An excellent way to practise free quilting is to stitch around the rose pattern in the fabric, aiming to stitch smoothly around the pattern. Nobody will notice the odd wobble and practice makes perfect. Once you have quilted the middle, change to a walking foot and place the left-hand side of the walking foot on the inside edge of the outer strips or against the picture, which will give a guide of about ½in (1.3cm). With stitch length 2, stitch around the edge of the middle square, keeping the left-hand edge as straight as possible (see Fig 2). Pull all the quilting threads to the back and tie off. On a quilt I always sew the ends in, but for this cushion I tied them.

4 Lay the cushion front and back right sides together and sew across the top (Fig 3). Take the lining strip and turn in one long side ¼in (6mm) twice. Lay this on top of the right-hand edge of the back/front piece and sew right across with ½in (1.3cm) seam. Press towards the lining.

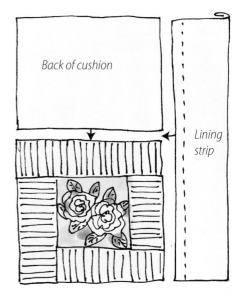

Fig 3 *Joining the back and lining strip to the front*

5 Fold the cushion in half with the lining stretched out and sew down the side and across the bottom (Fig 4). Clip corners and turn out. Push the lining in except for the last ½in (1.3cm) and top stitch in the seam ditch to keep the lining in place.

Fig 1 *Piecing the cushion front together*

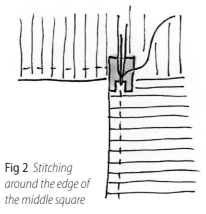

Fig 2 *Stitching around the edge of the middle square*

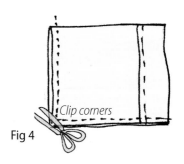

Fig 4

6 Take one of the tie strips and fold it in half lengthways (Fig 5). Sew across the bottom and up to the middle and then reverse back a few stitches. Start sewing again but leaving a gap of about 2in (5cm) and stitching down to the other end. Clip the corners, turn through to the right side using a pencil, slipstitch the gap closed and then press. Repeat with the other tie strip.

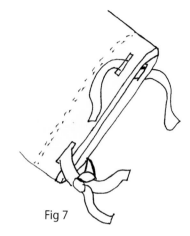

Leave gap

Fig 5 *Sewing the ties*

8 Insert the cushion pad into the cover and tuck the pad in under the lining to hide it. Feed the ties through the buttonholes and tie a loose knot (Fig 7).

Fig 7

7 On the right-hand side of the front and the back of the cushion, mark where you would like your two buttonholes to be, making sure that they line up on the front and the back pieces and are vertical (Fig 6). Stitch the buttonholes on your machine – these need to be about 1¼in (3.2cm) long, so the ties will feed through them. Consult your machine manual if need be.

Stitch the buttonholes

Fig 6 *Stitching the buttonholes*

Pie Crust Cushion

This cushion is really comfortable and one of my all-time favourites, inspired by the cows in our meadow and all the wild flowers that burst into flower year after year. I call it a pie crust cushion because it looks like a raised pie thanks to the gusset and the crimped edge. The front and back of the cushion are the same square size and can be made from either a single piece of fabric or from pieced shapes. The appliqué is worked using a needle-turn method and the floral fabric for the cow can be whatever you choose. Some easy hand embroidery creates a charming scene, and a button jar is very useful here, allowing you to dip in and find a selection of lovely old buttons. It's surprising how many you can source from recycled clothing and your granny's button jar!

The cushion can be made in different sizes. In a larger one you could have the gusset 4in (10.2cm) deep instead of 2½in (6.3cm) and perhaps include a zip in the gusset. You could also make a hard-wearing garden cushion from old denim or cord trousers and even include a pocket for tools.

Requirements

- Dark floral print for cow appliqué, about 10in (25.5cm) square
- Red fabric for heart appliqué, about 2in (5cm) square
- Light floral print for cushion front, fat quarter
- Blue ticking stripe fabric for cushion back, fat quarter
- Brown ticking stripe, about 8in (20.3cm) square
- Plain linen or floral fabric for gusset, long quarter
- Cotton wadding (batting), two 13in (33cm) squares
- Calico for lining, two 13in (33cm) squares
- Embroidery threads, selection of green, white, pale yellow and red
- Strong perle thread for edge sewing
- Assorted buttons
- Cushion pad, 14in (35.5cm) square
- Light box (optional)

Finished size: 12in (30.5cm) square

tip

The cushion pad needs to be larger than the finished size of the cushion cover to allow for the depth of the gusset. Buying a larger pad is cheaper and easier than finding a box-shaped pad.

PREPARING FABRICS

1 From the brown stripe fabric cut Piece A (see Fig 1), 4in x 7½in (10.2cm x 19cm) (width measurement is given first).
From the grey floral fabric cut Piece B, 4in x 3½in (10.2cm x 8.9cm).
From the blue stripe fabric cut Piece C, 9in x 10in (22.9cm x 25.5cm) (stripes horizontal).
From the grey floral fabric cut Piece D, 12½in x 2½in (31.8cm x 6.3cm).

2 From the blue stripe fabric cut a 12½in (31.8cm) square for the cushion back.
From plain linen or floral fabric for the gusset cut a continuous strip 2½in x 54in (6.3cm x 137.2cm), or piece together bits to this size.
From the wadding (batting) cut two 12½in (31.8cm) squares.
From calico cut two 12½in (31.8cm) squares for lining.

MAKING UP

1 Make up the cushion front (see Fig 1), joining Piece A to Piece B and pressing the seam towards A. Join Piece C and press C towards AB. Finally, add Piece D and press towards the top of the cushion.

2 To work the cow appliqué, begin by placing the cushion front face down on a light box and using the template provided trace the cow shape on to the back of the

pieced fabric, over striped Piece C. Make sure that the cow is traced as a mirror image, so it will be the right way round on the front of the cushion. If you don't have a light box then tape the fabric to a bright window.

3 Place the cow appliqué fabric right side up on the right side of the cushion front, making sure it covers the cow shape you have just drawn, and pin in place. Turn the work to the back and tack (baste) all around the outline of the cow through both layers of fabric. Turn the work to the right side and trim off excess appliqué fabric to within ¼in (6mm) of the tacked line. You can now needle-turn the appliqué in place. I started with the tail, then the body and then the head, leaving a little gap for the ears. For full details of this appliqué technique see General Techniques: Needle-Turn Appliqué.

4 Cut two ears from doubled fabric. With two ear shapes right sides facing, machine sew around with the curved edge using a small stitch length. Trim to ⅛in (3mm) and turn right side out, leaving a largish ⅛in (3mm) to tuck under the head.

5 To add a touch of warmth, add a red heart. Using the heart template provided cut out a heart from red fabric and stab stitch it in place near the cow's head.

tip — *I like to echo what I have on the front of the cushion with a little version on the back. If you want to do this then reduce the cow template to about half size and use this as the design on the back.*

Fig 1 *Piecing the cushion front by joining pieces A, B, C and D, ready to add the appliqué*

6 Make a quilt sandwich of the cushion front, the wadding (batting) and the calico backing and tack (baste) together ready to work the hand embroidery. I find it is easier to do the decorative stitching with the wadding in place as it gives something for the thread to 'bite' into. It also avoids the threads showing through on the right side if you are using a fine or pale fabric. Be careful not to pull too tightly though. Now make a quilt sandwich of the cushion back and the remaining pieces of wadding and calico and tack together, adding quilting if you desire.

7 Decorate the front of the cushion with hand embroidery using stranded cotton embroidery threads in colours to suit the fabrics. The design is meant to look like a wild flower meadow. You could use both

sides of the buttons to give a more antique look. Lightly mark where the flower stems are to be and mark buttons with a dot. Use backstitch for the flower stems, detached chain stitch for the leaves and daisy flowers, French knots in the daisy centres and buttons for the flower heads. Use whipped backstitch for the bird wings (a template is provided if needed). Stitch random red cross stitches under the heart. Use backstitches and long stitches for the cow's eyelashes. See General Techniques: Embroidery Stitches for working these stitches.

8 Add some quilting: sometimes I quilt around the cow but here I have only quilted along the seam. Quilting is very personal and on a cushion I sometimes quilt a lot and at other times not very much.

9 Now construct the cushion. For smaller cushions I just sew the pad in but you could insert a zip in the gusset if desired – see General Techniques: Inserting a Zip. Tack (baste) all around the edge of the cushion, front and back, to keep the corners in place when you sew the gusset on. Take the gusset fabric strip and place it face down on the right side of the cushion (Fig 2A). Place a pin ¼in (6mm) in from the corner. Leave the first 2in (5cm) unsewn, secure your start and then sew up to the pin. Raise the machine foot but leave the needle down in the fabric. With sharp scissors clip into the gusset only about ⅛in (3mm) at 45 degrees, towards the machine needle (2B). Remove the pin, rotate the work with the needle still in the fabric, and with your left hand pull the piece of gusset you have sewn upwards to make a right-angled corner (2C). Lower the foot and reverse stitch for two or three stitches, bringing the remaining long piece of gusset in line with the edge and then sew on (2D). Repeat this in all corners, until you are back to the start. To join the ends of the gusset, fold the unsewn 2in (5cm) piece forwards, butt it up to the gusset and sew together (Fig 2E).

10 Lay on the back fabric piece, right sides together with the gusset, and pin in the middle, matching the corners. Sew together around on the gusset side, repeating the clipping at the corners as before. Leave an 8in (20.3cm) gap in the bottom side of the cushion for inserting the pad later.

11 Turn the cushion right way out. With this cushion there is no need to neaten the edges or trim or clip because it all gets sewn into the 'pie'. Roll up your cushion pad and insert it into the cover carefully. Pin the edges of the gap together and slipstitch together. To create the slightly crimped edging, use a hand sewing needle and strong perle thread. Starting under a corner, begin with two over-stitches and then stab stitch around, slightly pulling or gathering so the edge resembles the crimped edge of a Cornish pasty (Fig 3). Do this on all the edges of the cushion.

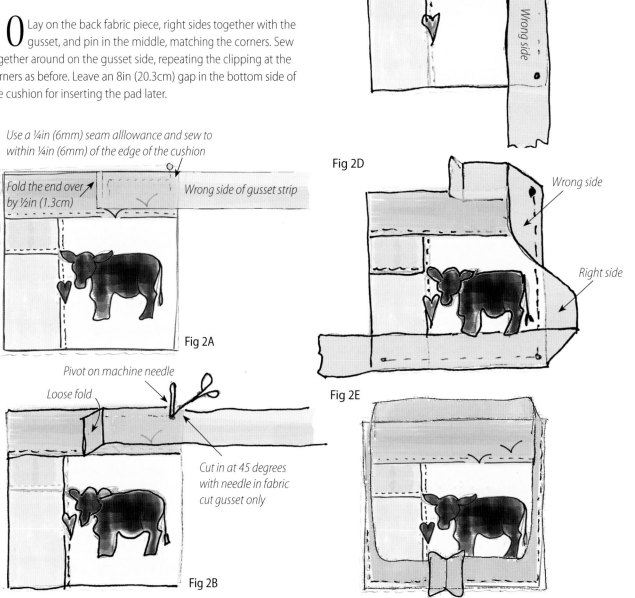

Use a ¼in (6mm) seam alllowance and sew to within ¼in (6mm) of the edge of the cushion

Fold the end over by ½in (1.3cm)

Wrong side of gusset strip

Fig 2A

Pivot on machine needle

Loose fold

Cut in at 45 degrees with needle in fabric cut gusset only

Fig 2B

Fig 2C

Right side

45 degree angle reverse back 3 or 4 stitches to secure

Wrong side

Fig 2D

Wrong side

Right side

Fig 2E

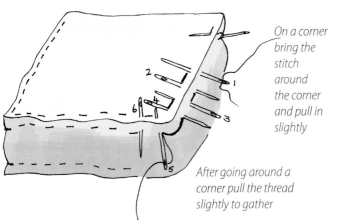

On a corner bring the stitch around the corner and pull in slightly

After going around a corner pull the thread slightly to gather

Fig 3 *Creating the crimped edging with stab stitching*

Heart Pie Crust Cushion

This cushion is made in the same way as the Pie Crust Cushion but with heart appliqués. Join sixteen 3½in (8.9cm) squares and press the seams open. I used an old ticking sample book and arranged the lines more or less randomly. Add 3½in (8.9cm) border strips to the sides and then to the top and bottom. The finished piecing is 18½in (47cm) square. Cut out the same size in plain linen for the cushion back. Using a needle-turn appliqué method and the heart template provided, draw around the heart shape on the back of each square and one in the middle of the back. Appliqué the hearts with a selection of patterned red fabrics. Add wadding (batting) and backing and hand quilt around the hearts. Add the odd button or two. Cut the gusset 3½in (8.9cm) and make up as in steps 9–11 of the Pie Crust Cushion.

Cornish Hedge Quilt

I call this my 'I love quilting 'til the cows come home' quilt. It evolved from a desire to use up scraps and strips of material and was inspired by the colours of the countryside and the tracks that animals make in the fields. The colours are very earthy and the quilting creates texture and interesting patterns. Quilts usually require perfectly matched seams, but a handy feature of this quilt is that the seams are staggered, to tie the pieces together in a similar way to building a Cornish hedge, so there are no seams that need to match.

Start by gathering muddy-coloured fabrics with different patterns, including plaids and checks. I included a touch of yellow to signify cowslips, and red for warmth. Of course, you can make this quilt in any colours you want – see an alternate colourway at the end of this chapter.

Requirements

- Fabrics made up of bits or scraps, about 2¼yd (2m) or equivalent to sixteen fat eighths
- A small picture or motif for the middle of the quilt (see Tip below)
- Wadding (batting) 55in (140cm) square
- Backing fabric 55in (140cm) square
- Quilting thread, either traditional waxed cotton such as YLI or Gütermann or cotton à broder for a more rustic look

Finished size: 50in (127in) square

To choose a range of fabrics it is sometimes helpful to find a picture in a magazine, or a piece of fabric that has a colour palette you like, and match the fabrics to the picture. You will be amazed how many colours and shades there are in one picture. Whether you like warm shades or cool, choose colours that make you feel good.

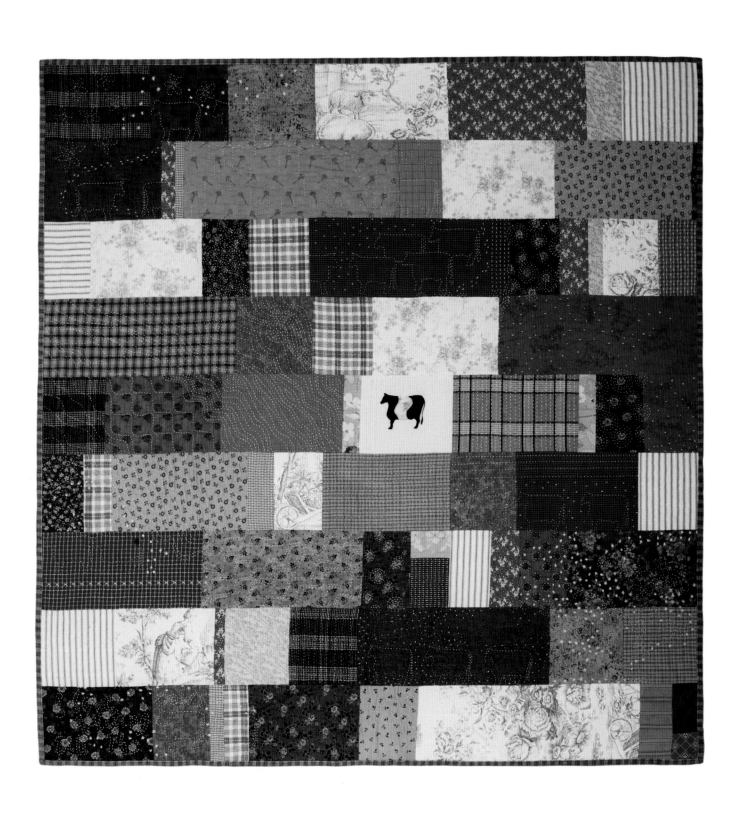

Cornish Hedge Quilt

PREPARING FABRICS

1 Using the rotary cutter but not adding seam allowances, cut strips 6in (15.2cm) wide across the width of your bits of fabric (you could cut each side of a 6in ruler if you have one). Just cut one strip off each piece to get started. If desired, you could join two pieces of fabric and then cut to the 6in, which means that you can use up small favourite pieces. I included the cow picture, but you could use a flower or a different picture or animal.

2 Cut each of the strips into three unequal pieces, which can be used in different rows of the quilt.

MAKING UP

1 Start by adding pieces to each side of the centre picture, using pieces all 6in (15.2cm) wide but in varying lengths of 2in (5cm), 3in (7.6cm), 4in (10.2cm), 5in (12.7cm) or 6in (15.2cm), mixing the sizes until the combined strip measures longer than 50in (127cm) – see Fig 1.

2 Start a new strip, laying it out and matching the overall length of the first strip but making sure that the seams do not match. Once you have made a few strips put them on a table or floor and lay the strips above and below the first strip. The strips can be moved left or right, arranging the colours to complement each other (Fig 2).

3 Make nine strips in total and lay them all out in a pleasing order, keeping the strip with the picture more or less in the centre. When you are happy with the layout, cut all the strips to 50in (127cm) long and sew them together using ¼in (6mm) seams, and working outwards with four strips each side of the central strip. Press all the seams open unless sewing by hand, in which case press both seams in the same direction. When sewing by machine I use stitch length 2: you should not see the stitches if the machine tension is correct.

Fig 1 *Joining pieces of varying lengths to make one long strip*

Fig 2 *Arranging the strips in a pleasing order but not matching the seams*

When quilting by hand I always use a 14in–22in (35.5cm–56cm) diameter hoop. If you are using a hoop it is very important to rest it on a table or chair to avoid strain on your back.

5 When the quilting is completed, bind the quilt to finish. I used a double-fold binding with a starting width of 2½in (6.3cm) – see General Techniques: Binding. Add a label to the back of the quilt, if desired.

4 Make a quilt sandwich of the quilt front, wadding (batting) and backing fabric (see General Techniques: Making a Quilt Sandwich). Start quilting from the centre outwards. I quilted around the cow and then worked outwards, using a quilting hoop to keep the layers flat. You could quilt up and down the rows of checks and around the flower shapes. I played around, sometimes matching the stitches row by row or deliberately mismatching them. This quilt is a good project to learn quilting, to practise making the quilting stitches and the gaps in between the same size – see General Techniques: Quilting.

Misty Morning on Bodmin Moor

In this version of the quilt I have used the colours from a springtime hedgerow on a misty morning. A good way to learn about colour is to find a photograph and match fabric colours to it. Remember that depth of shade can make a great difference to the look of a finished piece. For example, two pale or two dark colours can cancel each other out but a pale and a dark placed together emphasize the lightness and darkness and the shades will then jump out at you instead of blending in.

Ric-Rac Hare Cushion

This charming cushion is quick and simple and makes an excellent present. It features a lovely printed hare picture, which is perfect if you don't have time for hand appliqué. I love old fabrics and it is usually possible to find these vintage printed pictures – even old fabric sample books might have just the picture you need.

Instead of a hare you could use a flower picture, a dog, a horse, or whatever takes your fancy. Edging some of the patchwork with ric-rac braid adds a nice country look.

Requirements

- Spotty linen for cushion back, fat quarter
- Two different floral fabrics for the front (to complement each other and the linen), fat quarter of each
- Printed picture fabric at least 6½in x 5½in (16.5cm x 14cm)
- Ric-rac braid about ¾in (2cm) wide x ½m/yd
- Wadding (batting), about 13in x 18in (33cm x 45.7cm)
- Calico, about 13in x 18in (33cm x 45.7cm)
- Three medium and three small mother-of-pearl buttons
- Feather cushion pad 14in (35.5cm) square

Finished size: 16in x 11in (40.6cm x 27.9cm)

tip

Instead of choosing just one picture you could make a slightly bigger cushion and use several pictures – perhaps in a four-patch or nine-patch arrangement.

PREPARING FABRICS

1 From the picture fabric cut Piece A (hare motif) 6½in x 5½in (16.5cm x 14cm).
From floral fabric cut Piece B 6½in x 3½in (16.5cm x 8.9cm).
From floral fabric cut Piece C 6½in x 3½in (16.5cm x 8.9cm).
From floral fabric cut Piece D 3in x 11½in (7.6cm x 29.2cm).
From floral fabric cut Piece E 4in x11½in (10.2cm x 29.2cm).
From the second floral fabric cut Piece F 4in x 11½in (10.2cm x 29.2cm).

2 From spotty linen cut a piece for the back 20½in x 11½in (52cm x 29.2cm). For lining the buttonhole edge cut a piece of spotty linen 23in x 6½in (58.4cm x 16.5cm).

MAKING UP

1 Attach ric-rac braid to the top and bottom edge of Piece A, placing the ric-rac on the edge so it can be tacked (basted) in place straight down the middle (Fig 1). If you keep slightly less than ¼in (6mm) seam, when you add the next piece of fabric it should cover the tacking (basting) stitches.

2 Create the patchwork for the cushion front by sewing Piece B and Piece C to the top and bottom of Piece A (see Fig 2). Press away from Piece A. Now add Piece D, E and F, pressing all the pieces away from Piece A. You should now see half of the ric-rac neatly sewn in.

3 Take the pieces of wadding (batting) and calico and make a sandwich with the cushion front (Fig 3), with slightly more wadding and calico on the right-hand side. Tack around the edge a scant ¼in (6mm) to keep all the layers together. Trim to the edge of the front, leaving slightly more wadding and calico on the right-hand side. I didn't do any quilting on this cushion but you could quilt around the centre square and add buttons if desired.

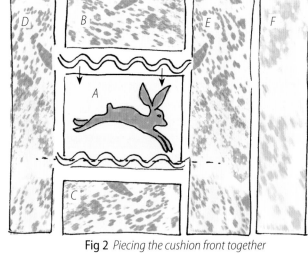

Fig 2 *Piecing the cushion front together*

Extra wadding on right side

Fig 3 *Making a sandwich of wadding and calico*

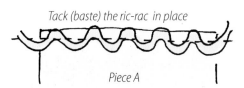

Tack (baste) the ric-rac in place

Piece A

Fig 1 *Adding ric-rac to the top and bottom of Piece A*

4 Take the cushion back piece cut earlier and join it to the top of the cushion front (Fig 4). Press the seam gently towards the back. Now take the lining piece and neaten one edge by turning in a ¼in (6mm) seam twice. Press the seam and then machine it with matching thread. Sew the lining to the right side of the opened-out cushion front using a ½in (1.3cm) seam (see Fig 4). Keeping the whole cushion out flat, fold the front and the back right sides together, matching the lining seam, and sew all the way down one side and across the bottom. You could neaten the edges using a zigzag stitch if desired.

5 Clip the corners and then turn right way out, pushing out the corners neatly. Push the lining inside except for the last ½in (1.3cm) and press gently. Top stitch to keep the lining inside. You can either machine or hand quilt close to the seam. Roll the cushion pad slightly backwards and insert into the cover. Shake gently to disperse the feathers.

6 Position the three medium buttons on the front of the cushion, about 1in (2.5cm) in from the edge, and align the smaller buttons with them on the back of the cushion (Fig 5). Use a strong thread (such as perle No. 8) to sew through both sets of buttons. If you prefer, machine sew buttonholes instead.

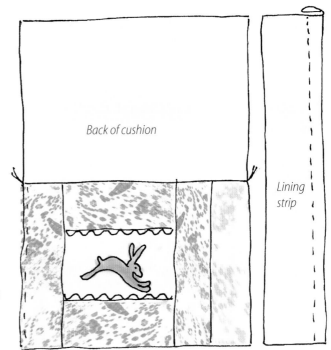

Fig 4 *Adding the back and lining strip*

Fig 5 *Sewing the button fastening together*

Vintage Frill Cushion

Old-fashioned flour sack or roller towel cushions are very attractive and suit the rustic, country-farm look I love. The fabric is simple but smart and also practical as it washes well. I just love the subtle reds and blues on this cushion and the frill adds an elegant look.

I made a feature of the little dot print and dark edge on the frill print, which resembles the coloured thread that manufacturer's used to put at the edge when weaving fabric, to measure how much cloth had been made. The self-cover buttons use the same fabric as the frill and add a decorative finishing touch but you could use any buttons.

Requirements

- Roller towelling or linen, 16in x 50in (40.6cm x 127cm)
- Print fabric for frill, buttonhole rectangles and covering buttons, ¼yd/m
- Lining fabric, 4½in x 16in (11.4cm x 40.6cm) (could be the same print as the frill)
- Ball of perle No. 8 thread
- Five buttons, self-cover or to suit fabrics
- Feather cushion pad 20in (51cm) square (will be folded)

Finished size: 15in x 20in (38cm x 51cm)

 tip

When making gathers you need to allow quite a lot of fabric, about two and a half or three times the finished length of the frill, depending on how close you want the gathers to be.

PREPARING FABRICS

1 Cut one piece from roller towelling or linen 16in x 47½in (40.6cm x 120.6cm).
Cut one piece from lining fabric 4½in x 16in (11.4cm x 40.6cm).
Cut one piece from print fabric for the frill 2½in x 42in (6.3cm x 106.7cm).

MAKING UP

1 Take the cut piece of roller towelling and mark it as follows (Fig 1). Measure along from the left-hand side 13½in (34.3cm) and put in a pin. Measure along 20in (50.8cm) and put in another pin – this will be the back shape. This will leave 14in (35.5cm) of fabric remaining. Mark this section with pins at 9in (22.9cm), 4in (10.2cm) and 1in (2.5cm). Press light creases at all the points marked with pins and then remove pins.

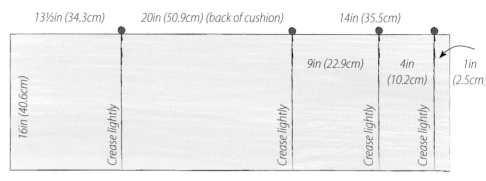

13½in (34.3cm)   20in (50.9cm) (back of cushion)   14in (35.5cm)

9in (22.9cm)   4in (10.2cm)   1in (2.5cm

16in (40.6cm)

Crease lightly   Crease lightly   Crease lightly   Crease lightly

Fig 1 *Marking the cushion fabric*

2 On the right-hand side turn the 1in (2.5cm) under and press to crease. On the left-hand side of the fabric, fold over the 13½in (34.3cm) piece on the first crease (see Fig 2).

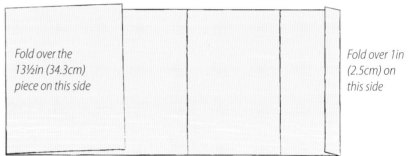

Fold over the 13½in (34.3cm) piece on this side

Fold over 1in (2.5cm) on this side

Fig 2 *Folding in at the sides*

3 To make the frill, take the long piece of frill fabric and iron a ¼in (6mm) hem twice on the right-hand side and sew under with matching thread (Fig 3). To create the gathers, take a ball of perle No. 8 thread, hold one end down a ¼in (6mm) in from the left-hand side edge of the fabric. Now zigzag stitch over the thread with your machine from A to B, being careful not to catch the thread. This is a much easier way to gather a piece of fabric than the usual two parallel rows of stitching, which can break just at the crucial moment.

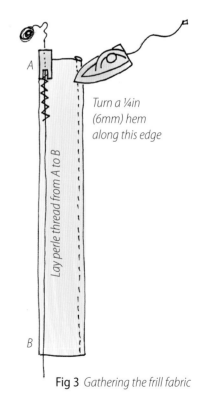

A

Lay perle thread from A to B

B

Turn a ¼in (6mm) hem along this edge

Fig 3 *Gathering the frill fabric*

tip *If you are using a fabric with a little pattern on the edge, position the pattern right on the edge when ironing the ¼in (6mm) hem.*

4 Pull on the perle thread to gather the frill so that it fits the left-hand side of the cushion front fabric. Lay the frill down right sides together with the cushion fabric and with the pleats pointing to the left as shown in Fig 4, and then machine tack (baste) into position.

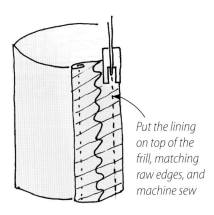

Fig 4 *Tacking (basting) the frill in place*

5 Take the 4½in x 16in (11.4cm x 40.6cm) piece of lining fabric and neaten one edge by turning a ¼in (6mm) hem twice on the right-hand side. Lay this lining fabric piece on top of the frill, raw edges matching and sew together with a slightly generous ¼in (6mm) seam (Fig 5). Using a slightly wider seam means that you do not have to remove the gathering thread, although you could pull it out if you prefer. Turn the lining to the back of the cushion piece and finger press in place; this will encase the frill neatly.

Put the lining on top of the frill, matching raw edges, and machine sew

Fig 5 *Sewing the lining in place*

6 Lay the back of the cushion cover on a table and fold in each side as shown in Fig 6. Mark the five buttonhole positions on the left-hand side and the five button positions on the right-hand side.

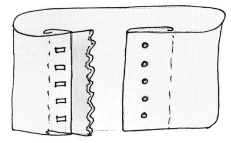

Fig 6 *Marking the positions of the buttons and buttonholes*

7 Prepare the buttonholes – I used bound buttonholes with rectangles of the print fabric. Set the sewing machine for 1¼in (3.2cm) long buttonholes or slightly longer than your buttons. Use the bound buttonhole function on your machine if you have it (see General Techniques: Bound Buttonholes). Sew the buttonholes and cut the slits. Push the rectangle fabric through the holes and neaten with small stitches.

8 Cover the buttons (if using this sort) using the same fabric as the frill – I used plastic self-cover buttons. See General Techniques: Covering Buttons.

9 Button up the cushion cover and put it right sides together. Sew a generous ¼in (6mm) seam down each side (Fig 7). Stitch twice where the frill is enclosed to reinforce that area. Clip the corners, open the buttons, turn through to the right side and press. Take the cushion pad and roll the top down towards the back and insert into the cover – it should fill the cushion snugly. (You could buy a rectangular cushion if you prefer.) When the pad is inserted you will need to plump it up, like kneading dough, to disperse the feathers equally.

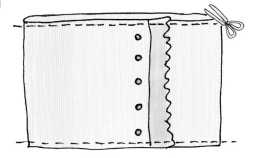

Fig 7 *Sewing the final seams on the cover*

Cornish Wave Cushion

The Cornish coastline of the United kingdom offers plenty of inspiration for quilters – the sea changes colour all the time and the boats sparkle in the sun as they glide over the water or bob around as they dodge each other. This cushion has a fresh, nautical feel, with its blue striped ticking and bright red sails on the boats.

   The cushion also makes good use of some old denim jeans. I used both sides of the denim to add contrast and echo the changing colours of the sea. Sometimes the seam of old jeans or the selvedge can be used to interpret a wave or ripples in the sea.

REQUIREMENTS
- Fabric with picture such as a boat or flag (Piece A), 6in x 8in (15.2cm x 20.3cm)
- Denim or old jeans: one piece 6½in x 3½in (16.5cm x 9cm); one piece 13½in x 4in (34.3cm x 10.2cm) and a piece at least 25in (63.5cm) square for the cushion back
- Gold or corn-coloured fabric for cornfields, 8in (20.3cm) square
- Small-print floral fabric for field, 6in (15.2cm) square
- Blue-and-white striped fabric in two different sizes of stripes for the water (or use sea-patterned fabric), fat quarter
- Dark blue fabric, 2½in x 13½in (6.3cm x 34.3cm) for sea
- Pale blue check fabric, 5½in x 4in (14cm x 10.2cm) for sea
- Dark blue spot fabric, 2½in x 4in (6.3cm x 10.2cm) for sea
- Navy blue plain cotton for boat hull appliqué, fat quarter
- Bright red plain cotton for boat sails appliqué, fat quarter
- Yellow fabric for the burgee appliqué on top of boats, about 12in (30.5cm) square
- Striped fabric for turn-in on right side of cushion and for binding, 6½in x 50in (16.5cm x 127cm)
- Fusible web for boat appliqué
- Calico, ½yd/m
- Cotton wadding (batting), ½yd/m
- Buttons for fastening, three large and three small
- Cushion pad 24in (61cm) square

Finished size: 24in (61cm) square

PREPARING FABRICS

1 Cut the following pieces of fabric for the piecing. The first measurement given is the width. The letters on Fig 1 indicate the various fabric pieces. Label your pieces once they are cut.

Cut Piece A from the picture fabric 7½in x 5½in (19cm x 14cm).

Cut Piece B from gold or corn-coloured fabric 2½in x 1½in (6.3cm x 3.8cm).

Cut Piece C small-print floral fabric 5½in x 1½in (14cm x 3.8cm).

Cut Piece D from denim 3½in x 6½in (8.9cm x 16.5cm).

Cut Piece E from denim 3½in x 6½in (8.9cm x 16.5cm).

Cut Piece F from denim 13½in x 4in (34.3cm x 10.2cm). If you use the frayed edge of the selvedge it will look like a wave when sewn in position.

Cut Piece G from blue and white stripe 5½in (14cm) square (with stripes horizontal).

Cut Piece H from gold or corn-coloured fabric 1½in x 5½in (3.8cm x 14cm).

Cut Piece I from denim 2½in x 5½in (6.3cm x 14cm).

Cut Piece J from blue and white stripe 8½in x 5½in (21.6cm x 14cm).

Cut Piece K from dark blue fabric 13½in x 2½in (34.3cm x 6.3cm).

Cut Piece L from denim 8½in x 2½in (21.6cm x 6.3cm).

Cut Piece M from pale blue check fabric 5½in x 4in (14cm x 10.2cm).

Cut Piece N from dark blue spot fabric 2½in x 4in (6.3cm x 10.2cm).

Cut Piece O from denim 7½in x 7in (19cm x 17.8cm).

Cut Piece P from wide blue and white stripe (with stripes horizontal) 14½in x 10½in (36.8cm x 26.7cm).

Cut Piece Q from denim 22in x 1½in (55.9cm x 3.8cm).

Cut Piece R from denim 1½in x 22½in (3.8cm x 55.9cm).

Cut Piece S from denim 2½in x 23in (6.3cm x 58.4cm).

Cut Piece T from denim 24½in x 3in (62.2cm x 7.6cm). This strip will be laid over the top of the block to use the selvedge edge.

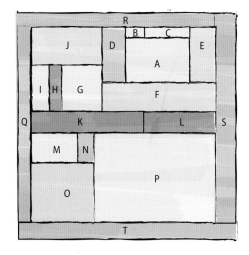

Fig 1 *Layout of the cushion front*

MAKING UP

1 Sew Piece B to Piece C, and then sew this BC unit to the top of picture Piece A, pressing the seam upwards (Fig 2). Sew Piece D to the left side of unit ABC and sew Piece E to the right side of unit ABC, sewing with the denim wrong side up for contrast (Fig 3). Press the seams away from the picture fabric. Sew Piece F to the bottom of unit ABCDE (Fig 4). If you are using the selvedge, don't sew a normal seam but lay it on top and sew across twice to secure.

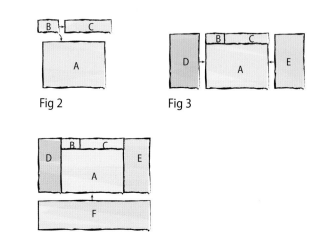

Fig 2   Fig 3

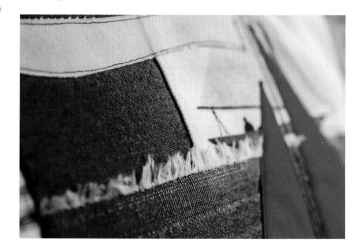

Fig 4

2 Sew Pieces G, H and I together, as in Fig 5. Press the seam away from the corn-coloured fabric. Sew Piece J to unit GHI, pressing up towards the denim.

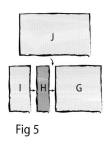

Fig 5

3 Sew the GHIJ unit to the left side of the ABCDEF unit and press towards the picture unit (Fig 6). This combined unit should measure 21½in x 9½in (54.6cm x 24.1cm), so trim slightly if necessary.

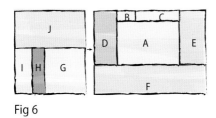

Fig 6

4 Sew Piece M to the left side of Piece N and then sew Piece O to the bottom of MN (Fig 7). Now sew Piece P to the right side of unit MNO and press the seam out towards the denim.

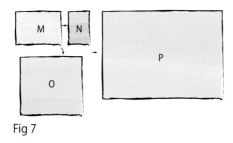

Fig 7

5 Sew Piece K to the left side of Piece L and then sew this unit to the top of unit MNOP (Fig 8).

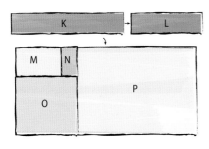

Fig 8

6 Sew unit A–J to unit K–P into one block (Fig 9). Sew Piece Q to the left-hand side of the block and Piece R to the top of the block. Sew Piece S to the right-hand side of the block. Sew denim strip Piece T to the bottom: don't use a normal seam but lay the piece over the top of the block so the selvedge edge is displayed, and then sew across it twice (Fig 10). The finished block should now be 24½in (62.2cm) square.

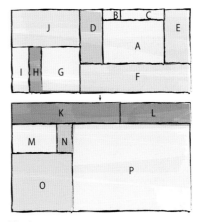

Fig 9

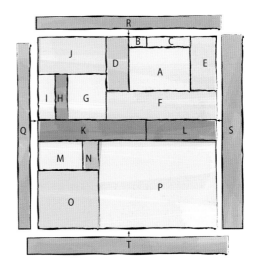

Fig 10

7 To add the appliquéd boats to the cushion front begin by backing the blue, the red and the yellow appliqué fabrics with fusible web (see General Techniques: Fusible Web Appliqué). Using the templates provided trace the boat hulls on to the paper side of the fusible web of the navy fabric, the sails on to the red fabric and the flags on to the yellow fabric. Cut out the shapes. Place all of the boat parts in position on the patchwork (Fig 11).

Fig 11 *Position of the appliqués*

8 Put the wadding (batting) and calico behind the cushion front and machine sew around the edge of the boat hulls, sails and flags with a straight stitch. I used dark blue thread for this and also for the 'masts' on the boats. You can then either hand or machine quilt, whichever you prefer. For example, I quilted the striped fabric pieces with wavy lines to represent waves on the sea.

9 Measure the cushion front and cut backing fabric the same size. I find the best way to do this is to lay your front piece on the backing and cut around. It needs to be fairly square and accurate.

10 Sew the front to the back along the top and then press the top seam gently (Fig 12). Open out and sew the 50in (127cm) blue stripe lining or gusset to the right-hand side, using a ½in (1.3cm) seam. Neaten one side of the strip by turning in ¼in (6mm) twice and then straight stitching along the seam. Press the lining to the back to make a crease line ½in (1.3cm) from the edge.

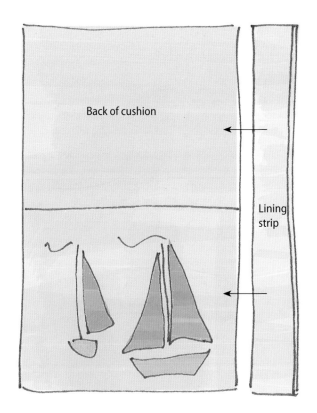

Back of cushion

Lining strip

Fig 12 *Adding the back of the cushion and the side lining strip*

11 Fold the cushion cover in half, with the lining out straight and matching the lining seams. Sew down the side and across the bottom, making sure that the seam matches where the lining starts. Clip the two corners and turn the cover right way out. Push the lining inside except for the last ½in (1.3cm) (Fig 13). Stitch in the seam ditch to keep the lining inside.

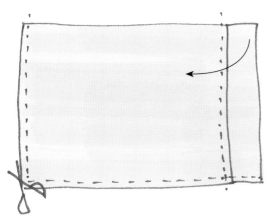

Fig 13 *Sewing the side lining*

12 Lay three large buttons along the open edge and mark the positions. Using a strong thread, sew on a large button, with a matching small one on the back, sewing through both buttons. You could leave the tied threads out on the right side of the buttons as a decorative feature if desired.

Flower Bed Quilt

Collecting fabrics is a passion for me and many people, and one that seems to grow and grow. We are so lucky today that we have so many fabrics available compared to when I started patchwork, but I always like to remember the origin of patchwork and use vintage and recycled fabrics when I can, as long as they are still strong. Many old quilts were created by using up shirt tails, cuffs and other fabric oddments, with 'frames' radiating out from the centre. This quilt follows that tradition.

I made two versions of this quilt, both using the same design: the pink one is hand quilted with cotton wadding (batting), while the blue one shown at the end of the chapter uses wool wadding and is beautifully long-arm quilted with feather patterns.

Requirements

- Eight prints with mixed pale floral backgrounds, fat quarter each
- Plain linen or fabric with a slight texture for Triangles A and Corners E, ¾yd/m
- Print fabric for Border 1 (rosebud), ½yd/m
- Pink striped floral fabric for borders half-square triangles and binding, 2⅛yd (2m)
- Pale background print to suit striped floral fabric, 1¼yd/m
- Cotton wadding (not too thick), 78in (198cm) square
- Backing fabric 78in (198cm) square (or join 15½in/39.4cm squares together for a pieced backing)
- Piecing cotton thread 50 weight in a colour to blend with fabrics
- Cotton perle No. 8 for hand quilting

Finished size: 72in (183cm) square

tip

If you find it hard to choose fabric colours, start with a piece of patterned fabric with several colours, or even a magazine picture, and then match the different fabrics to the original using a variety of florals, checks, stripes and spots in different scales.

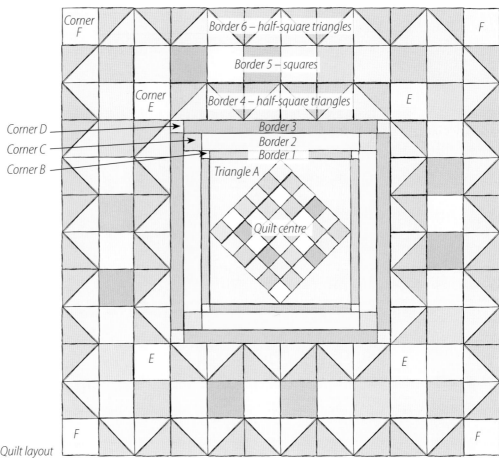

Fig 1 *Quilt layout*

Labels in figure: Corner F, Border 6 – half-square triangles, F, Border 5 – squares, Corner E, Border 4 – half-square triangles, E, Corner D, Corner C, Corner B, Border 3, Border 2, Border 1, Triangle A, Quilt centre, E, E, F, F

PREPARING FABRICS

1 From the mixed floral prints cut thirty-six 3½in (8.9cm) squares.
From the plain linen cut two 14in (35.5cm) squares. Cut them in half diagonally from one corner to another, to make four of Triangle A (includes seam allowance) – see Fig 1.

2 From print fabric for Border 1 cut four strips 1½in x 26½in (3.8cm x 67.3cm). From the pink rosebud fabric cut four 1½in (3.8cm) squares for Corners B.

3 From one of the floral prints cut four strips 3in x 28½in (7.6cm x 72.4cm) for Border 2.
From one of the floral prints cut four 3in (7.6cm) squares for Corners C.

4 From a floral print cut four strips 2in x 33½in (5cm x 85cm) for Border 3.
From one of the floral prints cut four 2in (5cm) squares for Corners D.

5 Border 4 and Border 6 are made up of half-square triangle units. From the pink striped floral fabric, cut one square about 42in (106.7cm) square and another square the same size from the pale background fabric. The half-square triangle units are made using a grid method, described in step 5 of Making Up.
From the plain linen cut four 6½in (16.5cm) squares for Corners E.
From one of the floral prints cut four 6½in (16.5cm) squares for Corners F.

6 From mixed floral prints cut thirty-six 6½in (16.5cm) squares for Border 5.

7 For single-fold binding cut fabric strips 1½in (3.8cm) wide and join together to make a total length of about 300in (762cm).

MAKING UP

1 To make the quilt centre, take the thirty-six 3½in (8.9cm) squares and arrange them in six rows of six squares. Using ¼in (6mm) seams sew the squares together into rows and then join the six rows together (Fig 2) – for details on this piecing and pressing see General Techniques: Cutting and Piecing: Squares and Rectangles.

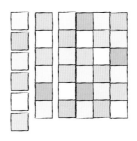

Fig 2 *Sewing the quilt centre*

2 Now take the four Triangles A cut earlier. With right sides together, pin two triangles on opposite sides of the quilt centre and sew together. Open out as shown in Fig 3 and press the seams towards the patchwork centre. You will notice that a little ear of fabric sticks out each end as if the triangle is too big, but this is needed to make a good cross-over when you sew the other triangles on. Add the other two triangles and press.

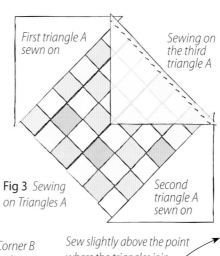

Fig 3 *Sewing on Triangles A*

3 Add Border 1 as follows. Take two of the 1½in x 26½in (3.8cm x 67.3cm) strips cut earlier and sew them to the top and bottom of the quilt. Make sure where you sew across the two joined triangles that you sew slightly high of the cross, so that when the fabric strip is pressed you will have a perfect point that is not clipped off (shown in red on Fig 4). For the other two 1½in x 26½in (3.8cm x 67.3cm) strips, sew a 1½in (3.8cm) square (Corner B) to each end of the long strips. Press the square towards the strip, so it will then butt up to the top and bottom border. Sew these strips to the sides of the quilt, matching seams neatly (Fig 5). Press towards the border.

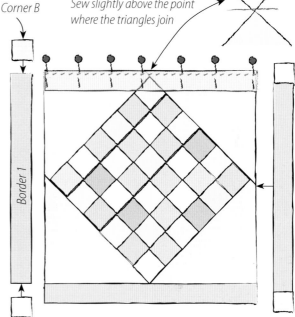

Fig 4 *Sewing on Border 1*

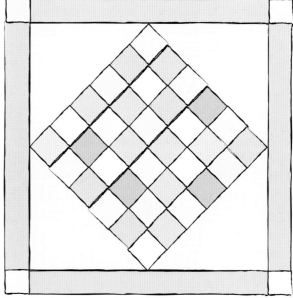

Fig 5 *Border 1 sewn in place with cornerstones*

Flower Bed Quilt

4 Using the relevant strips of fabric, sew on Border 2 and Border 3 in the same way, using the 3in (7.6cm) squares for Corners C on Border 2 and the 2in (5cm) squares for Corners D on Border 3.

5 Make the half-square triangle units for Border 4 as follows. I use a grid method (shown in Fig 6), which makes a total of seventy-two units. You require sixty-four units for the quilt, leaving you eight spare for a cushion or another project. This grid technique is not suitable for hand sewing as the stitching will be cut through. Take the two large squares of fabric cut earlier and steam iron them right sides together. Lay the paired squares flat on a table. Draw a grid on the fabric *as accurately as possible*, six squares wide x six squares high, each square 6⅞in (17.5cm). These marked lines will become your cutting lines after you have machined. Now mark all the diagonal lines across the grid. Pin about four pins in each square, away from where you are going to machine. Machine ¼in (6mm) *inside* each diagonal line, as shown by the red line on the diagram, pivoting with the needle down in the fabric when you meet the solid line. Repeat this carefully in each individual square. Do *not* cross into the next square – sew them all individually. You don't need to reverse or secure. Now stitch all the way around the outside.

6 Once you have stitched everywhere, cut on the solid lines. If you check before you cut you will see if you have machined in the wrong place as you will have a double square. Cut across the diagonal of each square (shown as a red line in Fig 7) to create two squares made up of two triangles in different fabrics. Press all the half-square triangles seams towards the pink striped floral fabric.

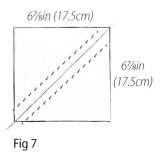

6⅞in (17.5cm)

6⅞in (17.5cm)

Fig 7

7 To sew Border 4, take six half-square triangle units, arranging them as shown in Fig 8, and then join the units together. Make two like this and sew them to the top and bottom of the quilt. Now make another two strips of six half-square triangle units. Take the four 6½in (16.5cm) squares of plain linen (Corners E) cut earlier and sew a square on each end of the half-square triangle strips. Join these strips to the sides of the quilt, matching and pinning seam junctions carefully and easing to fit (Fig 9). Press seams towards Border 3.

Sew ¼in (6mm) from the diagonal lines

Draw the grid and then mark all the diagonals

Fig 8 *Arranging the half-square triangle units*

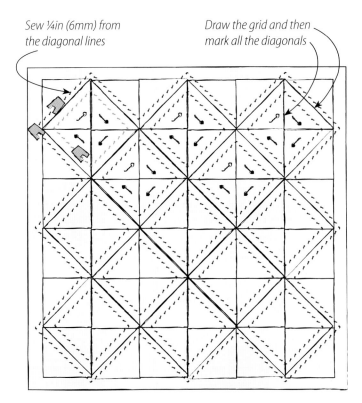

Fig 6 *Making half-square triangles for Borders 4 and 6*

Fig 9 *Adding Border 4*

8 To sew Border 5, take the thirty-six 6½in (16.5cm) squares cut earlier and join them together in two rows of eight squares and two rows of ten squares. Sew the shorter rows to the top and bottom of the quilt. Join the longer rows to the sides of the quilt, matching the corner seams carefully (Fig 10). Press seams outwards.

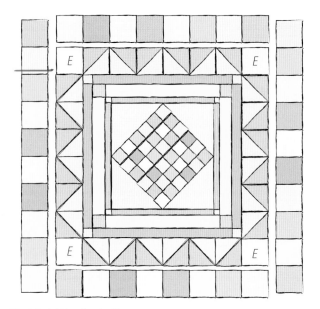

Fig 10 *Adding Border 5*

9 To sew Border 6, take forty of the half-square triangles made earlier and arrange into four rows of ten units, creating the same zigzag pattern as Border 4. Sew a row to the quilt top and bottom. Take the Corner F 6½in (16.5cm) squares and sew one square on each end of the other half-square triangle rows (Fig 11). Join these strips to the sides of the quilt, matching and pinning seam junctions carefully and easing to fit. Press the seams towards Border 5.

Fig 11 *Adding Border 6*

10 Prepare the quilt for quilting, referring to General Techniques: Making a Quilt Sandwich. For the quilting on the pink version of the quilt I used a daisy template and perle cotton No. 8 to quilt random daisies all over the centre and then moved on to a bigger daisy template in the border squares (Fig 12). I positioned the template over the joins to help blend all the elements together. If you prefer you could just outline quilt the patchwork shapes. For quilting advice see General Techniques: Quilting.

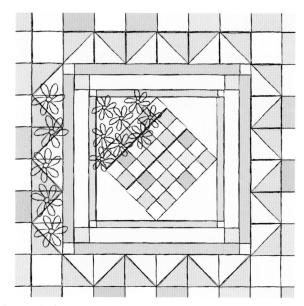

Fig 12 *Quilting*

11 When the quilting is completed, bind the quilt to finish. I used a single-fold binding with a starting width of 1½in (3.8cm) – see General Techniques: Binding. Add a label on the back of the quilt if desired.

Faded Flower Bed Quilt

This lovely blue version of the quilt is made in exactly the same way as the pink version. It uses our own sheep's wool wadding (batting) and has been gorgeously long-arm quilted with traditional feather patterns that were designed and hand drawn to fit the quilt.

Cowslip Country Cushion

This cushion is great fun and incorporates my love of horses, dogs, flowers, the countryside and of course quilts. Friends say that they have a vision of me sitting on the farm quilting among the daisies, so here it is – but with me driving off into the sunset! The cushion captures the colours of the fields, my grey mare, Silver Spice, and my dogs Mr T and Winston, who are always close by. I think the seasons can very much affect how you see colour and use fabric, so if you want to use brighter fabrics and more colourful embroidery that's fine – we all have our personal colour comfort zone. Feel free to adapt the piecing and appliqué shapes to suit your own design style.

This cushion is ideal for using up small bits of fabric from your scrap bag as many of the appliqués are quite small. The appliqué was applied using a needle-turn method but you could use fusible web if you prefer. The narrow border can be made from floral scraps cut into 1½in (3.8cm) strips.

Requirements

- Selection of green fabrics for fields and hedges patchwork, 12in (30.5cm) squares
- Blue ticking stripe, fat quarter
- Denim for outer border and overlapped back, 1yd/m
- Grey fabric for horse appliqué, 12in (30.5cm) square
- Scraps of fabric for dog appliqués and rug appliqué
- Fabric for cart appliqué (I used a grain-like check), 12in (30.5cm) square
- Red spotted fabric for dog collars, 2in (5cm) square
- Scraps of small floral fabrics for the quilt appliqués and narrow border
- Scraps of blue/black fabric for swallow appliqués
- Buttons for decoration, fifteen daisy buttons, plus a wooden heart, cotton reel and sewing machine buttons (see Suppliers)
- Blending thread for piecing, quilting thread in pale yellow and dark grey for reins
- Cotton wadding (batting) 25in (63.5cm) square
- Calico lining 25in (63.5cm) square
- Cushion pad 24in (61cm) square
- Light box (optional)

tip

Everyone seems to collect buttons and this cushion is a good opportunity to use them. Using little buttons for flowers is also quicker than appliquéing them and can create an instant wildflower meadow.

Finished size: 24in (61cm) square

PREPARING FABRICS

1 Refer to Fig 1 and Fig 6 when cutting the fabrics. Cut Piece A (pale green floral), 11in x 6½in (27.9cm x 16.5cm).
Cut Piece B (blue/green floral), 11in x 8½in (27.9cm x 21.6cm).
Cut Piece C (light green floral), 6in x 4½in (15.2cm x 11.4cm).
Cut Piece D (mid green floral), 6in x 10½in (15.2cm x 26.7cm).
Cut Piece E (striped ticking), 2½in x 14½in (6.3cm x 36.8cm).
Cut Piece F (green check), 18½in x 4½in (47cm x 11.4cm).

2 Cut Piece G (floral strips joined together), 1½in 18½in (3.8cm x 47cm).
Cut Piece H (floral strips joined together), 19½in x 1½in (49.5cm x 3.8cm).
Cut Piece I (floral strips joined together), 19½in x 1½in (49.5cm x 3.8cm).
Cut Piece J (floral strips joined together), 1½in x 20½in (3.8cm x 52cm).
Cut Piece K from denim, 20½in x 2½in (52cm x 6.3cm).
Cut Piece L from denim, 20½in x 2½in (52cm x 6.3cm).
Cut Piece M from denim, 2½in x 24½in (6.3cm x 62.2cm).
Cut Piece N from denim, 2½in x 24½in (6.3cm x 62.2cm).

3 Cut two pieces for the overlapped back of the cushion from denim, each 19in x 24½in (48.2cm x 62.2cm).

MAKING UP

1 Following Fig 1 and using ¼in (6mm) seams, join Piece A to Piece B across the 11in (27.9cm) measurement and press the seam towards B. Join Piece C to Piece D across the 6in (15.2cm) measurement and press the seam downwards. Join unit AB to unit CD and press towards the left. Join Piece E to the right-hand side and press the seam towards the right.

2 Take Piece F and fray out about ½in (1.3cm) of the 18½in (47cm) width. Lay this piece on top of the A–E unit, overlapping ½in (1.3cm) of the bottom of A–E unit and stitch across twice to secure. This frayed edge will resemble grass. The rest of the piecing for the cushion front is done after the appliqué is finished.

3 To work the appliqué use the templates provided and refer also to General Techniques: Needle-Turn Appliqué. The full appliqué design is shown in Fig 2, with the three main stages of the appliqué shown in Figs 3, 4 and 5. Lay the drawing face down on a light box or against a bright window. Placing the drawing face down is essential so that the motifs will face the correct way on the finished cushion. Draw the design on to the back of the pieced unit, placing the horse's feet just above the frayed grass. A dotted line indicates where one motif needs to be placed under another.

Fig 2 *The appliqué design*

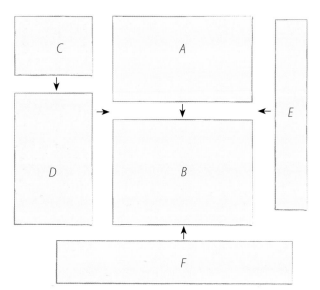

Fig 1 *Piecing A to F of the cushion front*

4 With an appliqué design such as this, with various motifs overlapping each other, you will need to sew the background motifs into place first – this is the first stage (Fig 3). To help you with this the pieces are numbered in the diagrams. Position the relevant appliqué fabrics, pinning and tacking (basting) them down. When positioning the appliqué fabrics hold the work up to the light to make sure you are totally covering the whole area and then tack (baste) on the line on the back with a contrast thread. Work in the order shown in Fig 3, starting with the horse's legs farthest away (1 and 2), the near-side blinker (3), the horse's tail (4), the top quilt (5), the girl's foot (6), the cart uprights (7 and 8) and the girl's hands (9). Where pieces are very close together you will need to tack on and sew them individually, so that each piece has enough seam allowance. This method keeps the work flat and is much easier and quicker than making loads of templates – I promise!

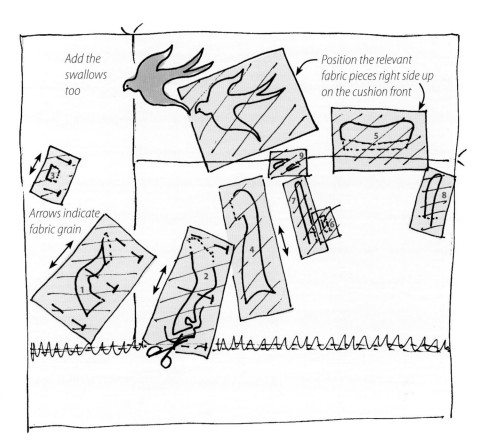

Fig 3 *First stage of sewing the appliqué motifs – suggested sewing order is shown by numbers*

5 The swallows can also go on at this stage. Tack (baste) and sew them one at a time. I used one piece of blue/black material for the birds and created the white and terracotta markings (shown shaded on the template) by embroidering a few straight stitches with sewing thread.

The bird tails are rather fine so if you prefer to use fusible web to bond them in place that's fine. In the old days, ladies used to demonstrate their sewing skills by showing how fine a point they could make with hand-sewn appliqué – pre-television entertainment of a sort!

6 Now move on to the second stage, adding the pieces shown in Fig 4. The numbers in green indicate pieces already sewn in place. The suggested sewing order is: the rest of the quilts (10, 11, 12, 13, 14), the black dog's body (15), the black dog's back leg (16), his ear (17), the cart (18), the dog blanket (19), the horse body (20), the horse neck and head (21), the horse blanket/breeching (22), horse mane (23 and 24), collar (25), blinker (26), forelock (27) and harness (28). When appliquéing the little quilts you do not need to sew the bottom of each one, as the next one will cover it. You could pad the quilts slightly by tucking in some wool or fluffed up wadding.

Fig 4 *Second stage of sewing the appliqué motifs. Numbers in green indicate pieces already sewn in place. Add pieces 10–28, as numbered*

7 Now move on to the third stage, adding the pieces shown in Fig 5. The suggested sewing order is: blanket under the gold dog (29), dog's body (30), head (31), ear (32), neckerchief (33), back leg (34), tail (35) and the black dog's collar (36). The girl's foot/leg and two hands are already in position, so now add the jeans (37), head (38), back arm (39), jacket (40), front arm (41), hair (42) and scarf (43).

8 For the wheel, place a piece of fabric right side up on top of the right side of the cushion and tack (baste) around the inner and outer circle of the wheel. Remember that shape of your tacking will be the final appliqué shape, so draw around a cup if you want a perfect circle. Starting on the outside of the wheel, trim back to ³⁄₁₆in (5mm) or a small ¼in (6mm), and appliqué under. Do the same to the inner line, which finishes off the ends of the spokes. I sewed a button in the middle to cover the other end of the spokes. The last piece of appliqué is the shaft that holds the horse and cart together. I put my checked fabric diagonally as it's hard sometimes to keep checks straight in a longer piece.

The spokes are placed first and then covered by the wheel rim

Fig 5 *Third stage of sewing the appliqué motifs. Suggested sewing order shown by numbers 29–43*

I appliquéd the wheel spokes but you could embroider them using backstitch. If using embroidery, lay your fabric on top of the master copy and draw a gentle line on the right side for the embroidery placement. Alternatively, you could use very fine ribbon.

9 With the appliqué finished you can now continue the piecing of the cushion front. The narrow border is made up of Pieces G, H, I and J, which are created by sewing together random lengths of different fabrics, all 1½in (3.8cm) wide. Sew Piece G to the right side of the cushion front. Add Piece H, then I and finally J (see Fig 6).

10 For the final border, sew Piece K to the bottom of the cushion front and Piece L to the top. Sew Piece M to the left-hand side and Piece N to the right-hand side. The cushion front should now measure 24½in (62.2cm) square.

Fig 6 *Piecing the rest of the cushion front*

11 Make a quilt sandwich of the cushion front, the wadding (batting) and the calico and then quilt as desired. On this cushion I kept the quilting simple, with buttons used to enhance the design. I machine quilted the sun in pale yellow, with five lines radiating out. The lines were sewn straight with the walking foot. A darning or free-quilting foot was used for the circular stitching around the sun. The same pale yellow thread was used to machine quilt around all of the appliqués to give a sunny glow. Outlining shapes with machine or hand quilting makes them stand out more. I machine stitched the reins and the rings on the harness in grey.

12 Add the embellishments now, arranging and sewing on the buttons. These can be personal to you or you could copy what I have used. I just love the wooden sewing machine button on top of the quilts. Add some hand embroidered straight stitches to the flower buttons and any extra details you like, such as red stitches on the coat.

tip | *Don't sew the buttons on before you finish the quilting as they will be in the way and can get scratched or even broken.*

13 Now make up the cushion cover. Hand or machine tack (baste), using stitch length 5 and a walking foot, around the edge of the cushion top a small ¼in (6mm) in. Trim the wadding and lining to the edge of the cushion front.

14 Take the two denim back pieces cut earlier and sew a hem down one of the long edges to neaten. Lay the back pieces right side down on the right side of the cushion front and using your walking foot sew a small ½in (1.3cm) seam in from the edge all the way around, reinforcing where the backs cross over. Clip the corners, turn out and insert the cushion pad to finish.

Bolster Cushion

Bolster cushions have a traditional look and cosy feel and add an extra dimension to a sofa or garden bench. The design of this one is very striking thanks to the needle-turn appliqué flowers in a lovely cheerful red. A red and cream toile and a subtle ticking adds to the exclusive look, making the cushion suitable for use as an attractive decoration on a bed.

Buttons have been used as a fastening on the bolster but a zip could be inserted instead if you prefer. This cushion is made in a similar way to the Pie Crust Cushion but in a horizontal, cylindrical format.

Requirements

- Ticking fabric (sand stripe), ½yd/m
- Toile or patterned print, ½yd/m
- Green fabric for appliqué flower stems, fat quarter
- Pale red fabric for appliqué flowers, fat quarter
- Strong yellow fabric for flower centres, 6in (15.2cm) square
- Three large buttons
- Cotton wadding (batting), ½yd/m
- Lining or calico, ½yd/m
- Cotton ric-rac in a colour to suit your fabrics, 1in (2.5cm) wide x 2yd (1.75m)
- Perle cotton No. 8 in red and machine quilting threads to suit your fabrics
- Bias maker (optional)
- Bolster cushion pad, 20in (51cm) long x 9in (23cm) diameter

Finished size: 20in x 9in (51cm x 23cm)

tip

The ric-rac braid is decorated with hand embroidery but instead of working cross stitches over the ric-rac you could use very small buttons if you prefer.

PREPARING FABRICS

1 Cut one piece from ticking, using stripes horizontally, 14½in x 32½in (36.8cm x 82.5cm).
Cut two pieces from toile print, each 4½in x 32½in (11.4cm x 82.5cm).
Cut three strips of green fabric on the bias, each 1in x 20in (2.5cm x 50.8cm).
Cut two circles from toile print, each 9½in (24.1cm) diameter.
Cut two pieces from toile print, each 3in x 21in (7.6cm x 53.3cm), for binding.

2 Cut two wadding (batting) circles, each 9½in (24.1cm) diameter.
Cut two circles from calico for lining, each 9½in (24.1cm) diameter.
Cut two lengths of cotton ric-rac, each 32½in (82.5cm) long.

MAKING UP

1 To piece the cushion, take the two 4½in x 32½in (11.4cm x 82.5cm) pieces of toile and sew them to either side of the ticking rectangle. Make sure that any pattern on the toile is pointing in the same direction. Press the seams open.

2 Lay the lengths of ric-rac on each seam and machine sew down the middle with matching thread. Using red perle cotton sew random cross stitches over the ric-rac.

3 To make the bias stems for the appliqué, take the 1in x 20in (2.5cm x 50.8cm) strips of green fabric and use a bias maker to turn in the edges, as follows. With the right side of the fabric facing down, thread or push the strip through the bias maker. Start to pull the folded strip out of the bias maker, using the point of a steam iron to press the folded strip (see Fig 1). The two edges will turn in, almost touching each other, and this will create a finished bias binding ½in (1.3cm) wide.

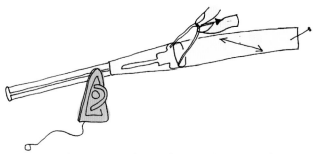

Fig 1 *Using a bias maker to make bias tape for stems*

4 Place the bias strips on the pieced cushion front, curving the stems as shown in Fig 2. Note that the join in the cushion will be at the bottom. As you position the stems, hold them in place with little appliqué pins. Now sew the stems in place with matching thread and tiny stitches (Fig 3).

Fig 2 *Positioning the stems*

Fig 3 *Sewing the stems*

5 To work the flower appliqués, use the large and small daisy templates and position the flowers as shown in Fig 2. Using needle-turn appliqué, sew on one big daisy and two smaller ones, using matching thread and small appliqué pins. Appliqué the yellow circles in the flower centres. For details on this technique see General Techniques: Needle-Turn Appliqué).

6 When the appliqué is finished, place your finished cover on to the cotton wadding (batting) and calico and quilt as desired. I used machine stitching in gold to add details to the flowers and added some leaf patterns in green randomly along the stems. Two leaf templates are provided for you to copy if you wish.

7 To make the rounded ends of the bolster, place a circle of wadding (batting) on top of a circle of calico and then a circle of toile fabric on top and tack (baste) them together close to the edge. Trim the circular sandwich around the edge, close to the toile fabric. Make a sandwich of the other three circles.

8 Take the two 3in x 21in (7.6cm x 53.3cm) pieces for binding and iron in half lengthways. Lay one piece on top of one of the short ends of the cushion, face down to the right side, with cut edges together. Using a walking foot, stitch together, trim and then roll the folded edge to the back and slipstitch down (Fig 4). Tack (baste) each long edge, to keep the layers in place. Repeat with the other binding strip on the other short end of the cushion.

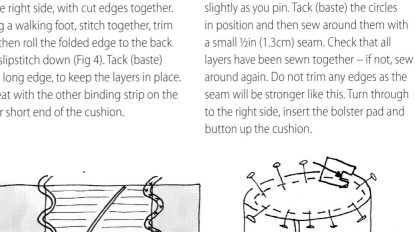

Fig 4 *Adding the binding*

9 Now overlay the edges of the short sides of the cushion by 2½in (6.3cm) and mark the buttonhole positions (Fig 5). Sew the buttonholes. Mark the positions of the buttons and sew in place. To strengthen the cushion sew 2in (5cm) in from each side.

Sew here to strengthen

Fig 5 *Sewing the buttonholes and buttons*

10 Turn the cover inside out. Take the circles prepared earlier and pin them right sides facing in, with the pins facing out (Fig 6). You might need to ease slightly as you pin. Tack (baste) the circles in position and then sew around them with a small ½in (1.3cm) seam. Check that all layers have been sewn together – if not, sew around again. Do not trim any edges as the seam will be stronger like this. Turn through to the right side, insert the bolster pad and button up the cushion.

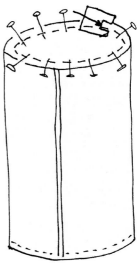

Fig 6 *Sewing the circular ends in place*

11 On the cushion edges pinch a generous ½in (1.3cm) and sew through using perle or strong thread, slightly gathering the fabric edge (Fig 7). This creates a crimped edge and gives a very nice finish.

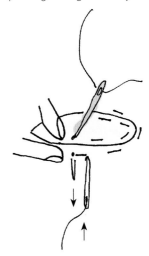

Fig 7 *Adding the edge stitching*

Rose Basket Cushion

The memory of the delicate colours of old-fashioned roses and their scent on the summer breeze is something to cherish, and I always think that roses are at their best just before the petals fall. This pretty cushion has an appliquéd basket of roses surrounded by other flowers and embroidered lavender, and is a way to keep roses looking lovely forever. I used the same print for all of the roses but you could vary the fabrics if you prefer.

Requirements

- Plain linen 1yd/m
- Dot or small print fabric, 12½in (31.7cm) square
- Coordinating striped fabric, ¼yd/m (long quarter)
- Pale small print or textured cotton for roses, fat quarter
- Scraps of various greens for rose leaves
- Pale yellow for daisy appliqués, fat eighth
- Contrast colour for daisy centres, 6in (15.2cm) square
- Check fabric or patterned fabric for basket, 8in (20.3cm) square
- Scrap of black fabric for swallow appliqué
- Stranded embroidery cotton in green and lavender
- Quilting threads to suit your fabrics
- Fine polyester or wool wadding (batting), 11in (28cm) square and 21in (53.3cm) square
- Calico, 11in (28cm) square and 21in (53.3cm) square
- Cushion pad 18in (45.7cm) square

Finished size: 20in (50.8cm) square, including edge

tip

The little folded fillets that edge the central panel use a striped fabric. A different part of the same fabric has been used on the outer border, which makes economical use of the fabric.

PREPARING FABRICS

1 For the background draw a 10in (25.4cm) square on the back of the dot or small print fabric but cut out a 12½in (31.7cm) square. This larger size allows for the edges fraying as the appliqué is worked and will be trimmed down to 10½in (26.7cm) later.

2 From plain linen cut Piece A, 10½in x 4½in (26.7cm x 11.4cm) – see Fig 8. From plain linen cut Piece B, 4½in x 14½in (11.4cm x 36.8cm). From plain linen cut Piece C, 14½in x 4½in (36.8cm x 11.4cm). From plain linen cut Piece D, 4½in x 18½in (11.4cm x 47cm). From plain linen cut four of Piece E (fillet pieces) each 1in x 11in (2.5cm x 28cm). From striped fabric cut Piece F, 18½in x 1½in (47cm x 3.8cm). From striped fabric cut Piece G, 18½in x 1½in (47cm x 3.8cm). From striped fabric cut Piece H, 1½in x 20½in (3.8cm x 52cm). From striped fabric cut Piece I, 1½in x 20½in (3.8cm x 52cm).

3 From plain linen cut two pieces for the cushion back, each 13½in x 20½in (34.3cm x 52cm). From striped fabric cut one strip 3in x 21in (7.6cm x 53.3cm) for binding one outside edge of the cushion back.

tip *When making the rosebuds, select a thin fabric as this will fold more easily. If you choose a fabric that is shaded in colour, rather than a plain solid, this will help to create more depth to the appliqué shape.*

MAKING UP

1 To prepare the fabric for the appliqué, use the templates provided and follow step 1 in General Techniques: Needle-Turn Appliqué. When the appliqué design is drawn, turn the drawing and fabric right way up to gently sketch on the lavender, which will be embroidered from the right side.

2 Take the fabric for the basket appliqué and pin it on the right side of the background fabric. From the back, tack (baste) on the drawn line as carefully as possible. Tack on the handle pieces that show between the flowers and the basket body. Trim away to a small ¼in (6mm) and sew under all round, leaving the small ends of the handle open – they will be covered by flowers later (Fig 1). Sew along the top of the basket and down the sides. Take another piece of basket fabric and tack on the basket base, trim and sew under.

Fig 1 *Preparing the basket appliqué*

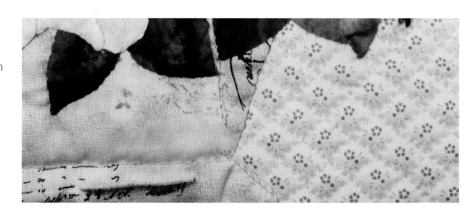

3 Make three rosebuds, as follows. Take a 2in (5cm) diameter circle of rose fabric, fold it almost in half with the straight grain diagonally across the circle (Fig 2A). Fold the right-hand side over to the left, so the folds are almost on top of each other. Run a small running stitch along the bottom raw edge and pull up tight (Fig 2B). Having the bias diagonally means the rosebud crinkles up nicely. Wrap the thread around twice to secure and then cut the bottom into a point so that it will fit into a rosebud holder when you add them later (Fig 2C).

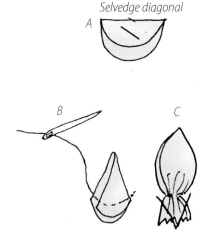

Fig 2 *Sewing the rosebuds*

4 Using the templates and the leaf fabric, follow the same appliqué technique for the leaves. Tack (baste) on leaves 1, 2 and 3 where shown on Fig 3 and sew under. Position leaf 4 slightly over part of leaf 3.

When appliquéing leaves I try to have the fabric grain running from point to point of the leaf, to encourage the fabric to lie flat. Sometimes there is a bit of fabric design I particularly want, in which case I ignore the grain on very small pieces.

tip

Fig 3 *Appliquéing the leaves*

5 Use the same appliqué technique and the swallow fabric to tack (baste) on the silhouette and sew under with matching thread.

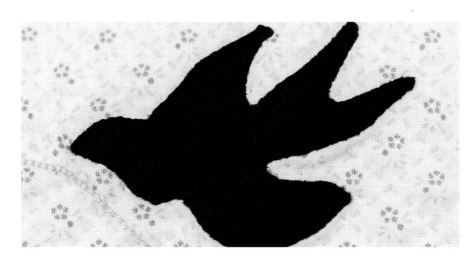

Fig 4 *Appliquéing the swallow and rosebud holders*

6 Tack (baste) on the rosebud holders in the positions shown in Fig 4. Sew up the right side to the red star on the right shown on Fig 5A and then down the left side from the left-hand red star. Before finishing off your thread add three or four little stitches as rose hairs. Leave the top of the bud unsewn and cut straight down the middle to about two threads from the middle dip (5B). Take the rosebud made earlier and insert small, closed scissors gently in the bud. Put the rosebud down into the bud holder and then finish sewing around (5C).

Sew up each side to the red stars

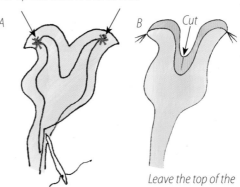

A   B   *Cut*   C   *Fitting the rosebud into the holder*

Leave the top of the bud unsewn and cut down the middle

Fig 5 *Sewing the rosebud holders*

7 Using the templates provided and the rose fabric, start sewing on the roses petal by petal, starting on the outside and working all the way around and then into the middle row (see Fig 6A–E). For the centre or stamen choose a fine spotted fabric or embroider dots for the stamens. I used a calico damask that had markings on it as I wanted the roses to look faded, but you could use stronger fabrics if you prefer.

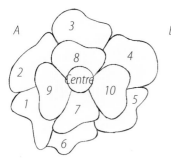 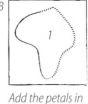 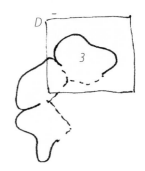 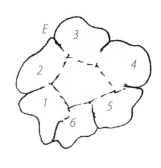

Add the petals in order from 1 to 10

Fig 6 *Appliquéing the roses*

You could embroider a poem or piece of prose by hand or machine for a charming country touch to your cushion. For example, there is space above the basket to write, 'The scent of an English summer gently blows in the breeze'.

tip

8 Now appliqué the daisies. Tack (baste) on petal by petal and sew under, leaving the ends pointing towards the flower centre unsewn. Make a little fabric circle (see General Techniques: Appliqué: Needle-Turning a Circle). Sew down with matching thread, tucking in the spare at the back to make the centre slightly raised.

9 If you have not yet drawn on the lavender, place your appliqué gently over the drawing and draw lines for the lavender. Use a small backstitch for the lavender stem and embroider the heads with a sloping stitch (I used a hand-dyed hemp thread). In the middle of the basket stitch lavender heads without stems.

10 To make up the patchwork of the cushion, start by adding the four Pieces E to the centre square of the cushion as follows. Fold all four pieces in half lengthways and press with steam. Place one fillet on the top of the centre square and one on the bottom and tack (baste) on the edge of the fillet to the edge of the square (Fig 7). If you tack less than ¼in (6mm) you won't need to remove the tacking but it is essential to tack to keep the fabric pieces straight. Add the other two fillets and tack again.

Fig 7 *Adding four of Piece E to the centre panel*

11 These little fillets are kept in place by pieces A, B, C, and D (Fig 8). Sew these pieces on in A, B, C, D order and press seams outwards. Now sew on the outer border pieces F, G, H and I.

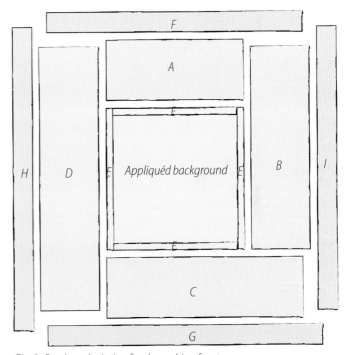

Fig 8 *Patchwork piecing for the cushion front*

12 Place the cushion front on the smaller square of wadding (batting) and then add the larger square of wadding and the backing fabric – this gives the cushion front a nice padded look. I used a fine wool wadding and fine calico so that I could quilt with small hand stitches. I did not mark the block but just quilted between the lines by eye, which gives a really lovely texture and is very traditional. Quilt right up to and under the little fillet.

13 Make up the cushion cover using an Oxford-style case – see General Techniques: Making an Oxford-Style Cushion Cover. Use the striped strip cut earlier to bind one long edge.

14 Stitch in the ditch (in the seam line) between the striped outer border and the plain linen border, by hand or machine. This makes the finished size of the cushion 18in (45.7cm) square and creates a very nice flanged edge.

Wobbly Dog Quilt

This quilt, with its gentle curves and wobbly dogs, evolved when some lovely 'sherbet pips' fabric came into our shop. It would make a lovely quilt for a child, or even a pampered pooch! The dogs appear as appliqué and also as a hand-quilted motif. Both sides of some denim fabric have been used alternately to create more visual interest and the blues work well with the red and grey fabrics. Layering your block fabrics, so several shapes can be cut out at once, makes cutting the blocks faster and easier.

You could adapt this design and use a floral print instead of denim if you prefer and take a flower, bird or other symbol from the fabric as the basis of your appliqué design.

Requirements

- Pale blue lightweight denim (sometimes called chambray), 1¾yd (1.5m) – or two similar blues (see Tip)
- Red dog or patterned fabric for centre of some blocks and outer border, 1yd/m
- Grey dog fabric for some block centres and quilt back, 2¾yd (2.5m)
- Pictorial fabric, fat quarter
- Fabric for inner border 12in (30cm) x width of fabric
- Cotton wadding (batting) 52in (132cm) square
- Chocolate brown hand quilting thread
- Freezer paper 2⅛yd (2m)
- Masking tape
- Permanent marker pen
- Binding fabric, long ¼yd (0.25m)

Finished size: 48in (122cm) square

tip

For this quilt the denim fabric was used on the right side for some blocks and the wrong side for alternate blocks, creating a two-tone pattern. Check that your denim looks sufficiently different on both sides.

PREPARING FABRICS

1 From denim cut eight 11½in (29.2cm) squares with the denim's right side facing up and eight squares with the denim's wrong side facing up (or using two different blue fabrics).
From denim cut four 2in (5cm) squares for the inner border corners.
From denim cut four 4½in (11.4cm) squares for outer border corners.

2 From the inner border fabric cut four strips each 2in x 37½in (5cm x 95.2cm).
From the outer border fabric (red dog) cut four strips each 4½in x 40½in (11.4cm x 102.9cm).
From the binding fabric cut strips 1½in (3.8cm) wide and join to a total length of about 200in (80cm) for single-fold binding.

tip

*Rotary cutting is very helpful for this fun quilt, but take care as rotary cutters are **very** sharp. Keep yours safe in a little padded bag at all times when not in use. A bag also protects the blade, which means that it will last longer.*

MAKING UP

1 I used freezer paper as a template for cutting my fabric, including seam allowance. Copy pattern pieces A and B three times from the template provided (these are the blocks). Place freezer paper wax side down over each pattern, keeping it in place with masking tape. With a fairly thick permenant felt pen trace all the lines of the pattern on to the smooth side of the freezer paper (Fig 1). Using a fast-drying permenant marker will avoid any smudges or ink marking your fabric.

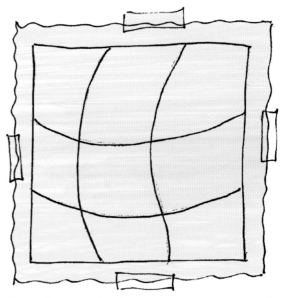

Fig 1 *Tracing Pattern Pieces A and B*   *Tape freezer paper over the pattern and trace curved lines and outer edge of block*

2 In the same way use smaller pieces of freezer paper wax side down over each A and B pattern, and trace only the AAA middle shape and BBB middle shape (Fig 2). Do this three times.

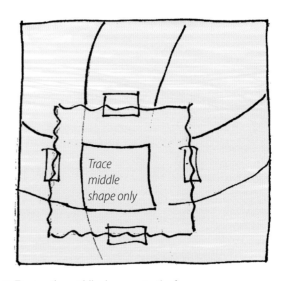

Trace middle shape only

Fig 2 *Tracing the middle shape on to the freezer paper*

3 Put three of the darker 11½in (29.2cm) squares of denim on top of each other, with edges aligned. Place the freezer paper pattern on top and iron in place with a hot, dry iron (Fig 3). Use your rotary cutting equipment to cut out the outer shape of the block. Repeat, to cut out a total of eight 11in (27.9cm) blocks in darker denim (Block A) and eight 11in (27.9cm) blocks in lighter (or reverse side) denim (Block B).

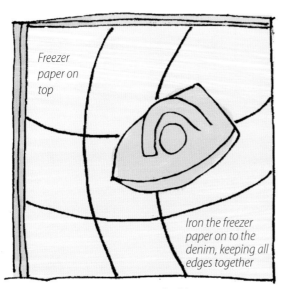

Freezer paper on top

Iron the freezer paper on to the denim, keeping all edges together

Fig 3 *Transferring the design to the fabric*

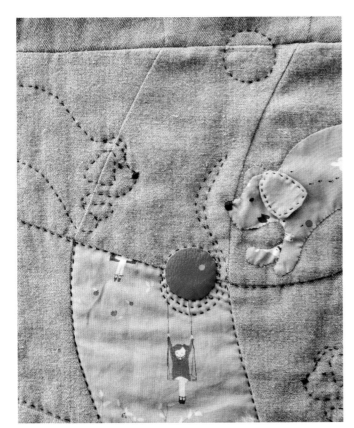

4 The curved lines of the block are now cut freehand with a rotary cutter on the black traced lines of the freezer paper square. Keep the denim squares in stacks of three and to keep all flat and square place your long ruler over part of the block and press down, keeping your fingers away from the edge (Fig 4). Cutting away from you, cut through the freezer paper along the curves lines, to cut the three blocks into their individual nine parts.

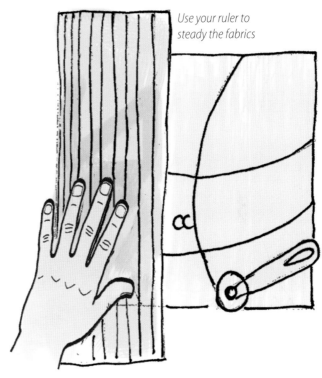

Use your ruler to steady the fabrics

Fig 4 *Freehand cut out the shapes of the block*

5 To create the different centres for each block, use the middle freezer paper templates made earlier. From red fabric cut two BBB middles and four AAA middles. From white fabric cut two BBB middles and one AAA middle. From grey fabric cut four BBB middles and three AAA middles.

6 Arrange the nine parts of each block on the floor or large table and take the middle shape out of each block (Fig 5A). In each block replace the centres of the A blocks with the AAA picture shapes and the B blocks with the BBB picture shapes (Fig 5B). Refer to the picture of the quilt.

Lay out each block and remove the centre

Fig 5A *Assembling the blocks*

Fig 5B *Replacing the centre shape*

7 Now join the blocks together as follows (Fig 6). Take your first block and join the three pieces in row 1, then the three pieces in row 2 and finally the three pieces in row 3. Press the seams in the rows in the directions shown in the diagram.

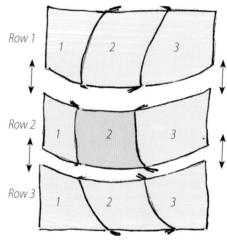

Row 1

Row 2

Row 3

Fig 6 *Sewing the blocks together*

8 Now join the rows together as follows. Lay row 1 on top of row 2, matching seams and pinning at the ends first and then at seam junctions. Sew with the seam curving up towards you (like a smile!), easing as necessary (Fig 7). Now sew row 3 to row 2 in the same way to complete the block. Repeat this to assemble all sixteen blocks.

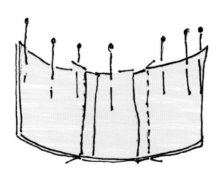

Fig 7 *Sewing the curved seams when joining rows*

9 Lay the blocks out starting at the top left-hand corner with a dark A block, alternating A and B blocks in each row as shown in Fig 8. Sew the blocks into four rows of four blocks, being careful to match and pin seams neatly. Now sew the rows together and press (Fig 9).

10 Add the inner border to the quilt as follows. Take two of the 2in x 37½in (5cm x 95.2cm) strips cut earlier and sew them to the top and bottom of the quilt. Take the other two 2in x 37½in (5cm x 95.2cm) strips and sew a 2in (5cm) denim square to each end. Sew these border strips to each side of the quilt, matching the seams as neatly as you can (Fig 10).

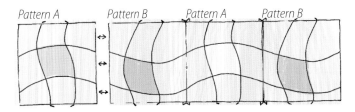

Fig 8 *Joining four blocks together*

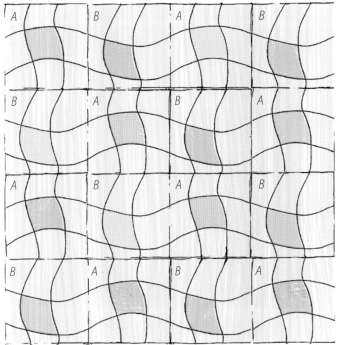

Fig 9 *Sewing the rows of the quilt together*

11 Add the outer border in the same way, using the four 4½in x 40½in (11.4cm x 102.9cm) strips and the four 4½in (11.4cm) squares.

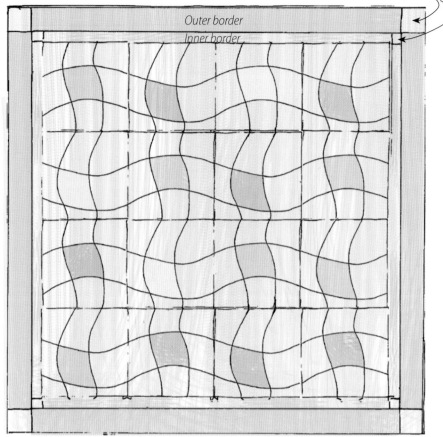

Fig 10 *Adding the borders*

12 To appliqué dogs use the template provided and draw the dogs in position on the back of the quilt. I made them look as though they were running along a path after a ball. I used needle-turn appliqué but you could use fusible web if you prefer (see General Techniques: Appliqué). I needle-turned the body in one shape and then added a three-dimensional ear. To make the ear, place the fabric pieces right sides together, draw around the ear template shape, and then machine around, leaving a little gap at the top. Cut out the ear shape with a scant ¼in (6mm) seam and turn the right way out. Tuck in the surplus fabric, top stitch or quilt around the ear and stitch on to the dog's head.

13 To appliqué the three balls, use red fabric and a circular card template about 1in (2.5cm) diameter (I drew around

a medium-size cotton reel) – see General Techniques: Needle-Turning a Circle. Appliqué the balls in place. I used the same circle for the quilting in the outer border.

14 Prepare the quilt for quilting, referring to General Techniques: Making a Quilt Sandwich. For the quilting I used the dog template and drew on more dogs, with their footsteps following the fabric lines. I started the quilting in the middle of the quilt and used a wooden quilting hoop, quilting the dogs and in the ditch, that is, away from where the seam has been pressed.

15 When the quilting is completed, bind the quilt to finish. I used a single-fold binding with a starting width of 1½in (3.8cm) – see General Techniques: Binding. Add a label on the back if desired.

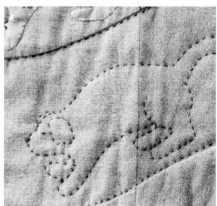

Daisy and Lavender Cushion

The use of pretty, floral fabrics, appliquéd daisies and embroidered lavender flowers remind me of looking across the garden on a summer's night. To make the lavender-coloured thread I sometimes mix thread colours or I use a hemp thread made by a friend, which is soft and resembles the lavender head. You could place a lavender or herb sachet inside the finished cushion to remind you of the summer scents.

The tied edge of this cushion is an attractive feature, inspired by the wool sacks on our farm. When we send the wool off to market we have to tie the edges of each wool sack together, and this rustic and old-fashioned look finishes this cushion off perfectly.

Requirements

- Linen or rustic cotton for piecing and for cushion back, 1yd/m
- Three or four floral prints, fat quarter of each (or cut different patterns from one fabric)
- White fabric for daisy appliqué, fat quarter
- Green fabric for daisy stems appliqué, fat quarter
- Yellow fabric for daisy centre, about 4in (10.2cm) square
- Wadding (batting), 25in (63.5cm) square
- Calico for lining, 25in (63.5cm) square
- Fusible web
- Sewing threads to match fabrics
- Machine quilting thread for daisy topstitching
- Embroidery threads for lavender, stranded cotton or perle
- Cushion pad 24in (61cm) square

Finished size: 24in (61cm) square

tip

For a quicker result you could find a printed fabric with a flower motif that can be cut out and appliquéd to your background. This type of appliqué is called broderie persé.

PREPARING FABRICS

1 Cut Piece A from dark floral print, 2½in x 6½in (6.3cm x 16.5cm).
Cut Piece B from floral print, 2½in x 6½in (6.3cm x 16.5cm).
Cut Piece C from a dark floral print, 6½in (16.5cm) square.
Cut Piece D from pale floral print, 10½in x 4½in (26.7cm x 11.4cm).
Cut Piece E from ticking stripe, 2½in x 10½in (6.3cm x 26.7cm).
Cut Piece F from floral print, 4½in x 10½in (11.4cm x 26.7cm).
Cut Piece G from plain linen, 4½in x 10½in (11.4cm x 26.7cm).
Cut Piece H from floral print, 16in x 4½in (40.6cm x 11.4cm).
Cut Piece I from plain linen, 2½in x 4½in (6.3cm x 11.4cm).
Cut Piece J from floral print, 2½in x 4½in (6.3cm x 11.4cm).
Cut Piece K from linen, 20½in x 6½in (52cm x 16.5cm).
Cut Piece L from linen, 20½in x 4½in (52cm x 11.4cm).

2 Cut Piece M from linen for the edge and folded-back lining 10½in x 50in (26.7cm x 127cm) (see Fig 6).
From bright floral fabric cut a piece 1in x 21in (2.5cm x 53.3cm) for the little insert or fillet. This is slightly long to ensure that the fillet is not pulled too tightly: it can be trimmed down later.
Cut a piece of linen for the cushion back 20½in x 24½in (52cm x 62.2cm).
From floral fabric cut one strip 2½in x 96in (6.3cm x 243.8cm) for the cushion ties – this could be different pieces joined together.

MAKING UP

1 Following Fig 1A, and using ¼in (6mm) seams, join Piece A to Piece B and then add Piece C, pressing seams open. Sew on Piece D and press open, being careful not to press out of shape. Add Piece E.

2 Continue with the piecing, adding Piece F and Piece G, pressing these seams towards the left-hand side (Fig 1B). Take the narrow fillet and press it in half along the length. Lay it on the bottom edge of unit A–G and tack (baste) in position about ⅛in (3mm) from the lower edge. It is very important to tack it in place, otherwise it will end up irregular.

3 Now join Pieces H, I and J together, pressing the seams away from I (Fig 1C). Add this unit to unit A–G: this seam will also sew the fillet into position. Finally, add Pieces K and L to the bottom and top, pressing the seams outwards. The piecing of the front of the cushion is now finished.

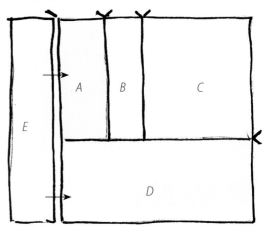

Fig 1A *Piecing the cushion front together*

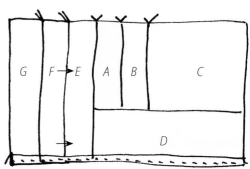

Tack the folded fillet in position along the lower edge

Fig 1B *Continuing the piecing*

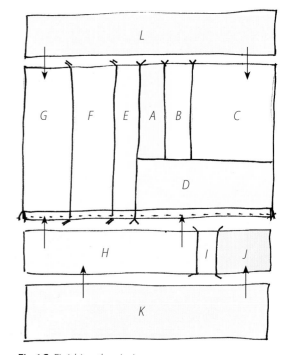

Fig 1C *Finishing the piecing*

4 Now you can begin the appliqué. To make the three flower stems cut three 1in (2.5cm) wide strips of the green fabric on the bias. You will need a total length of about 50in (127cm). Fold them in half lengthways and iron the fold. Lay the stems in position on the cushion front (see Fig 2) and using machine stitch length 1, sew them about ⅛in (3mm) from the folded edge (Fig 2A). Stitching this close to the folded edge will ensure that you can roll the fabric out over the curve. Using sharp scissors trim very close to the stitching (2B), then roll over the fold (2C) and either hand sew or machine sew the stem down (Fig 2D). This method creates lovely fine stems.

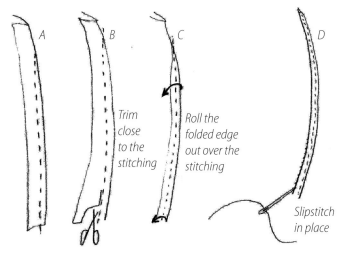

Trim close to the stitching

Roll the folded edge out over the stitching

Slipstitch in place

Fig 2 *Sewing the appliqué stems in place*

5 Using the petal templates and a fusible web appliqué method (see General Techniques: Fusible Web Appliqué), prepare the daisy petals. Lay the petals in position on the cushion front and bond in place. Fig 3 shows the approximate positions of the appliqués but you can vary this.

6 Cut calico and wadding (batting) for the cushion front, each 25in (63.5cm) square. Put the calico, wadding and cushion front together as shown in Fig 4. You will see at this stage that there is an extra 4in (10.2cm) of calico/wadding on the right-hand side. This will be used later when the long edge is added.

Fig 3 *Positioning the appliqué*

Extra calico and wadding on this side

Fig 4 *Adding the calico and wadding (batting) to the cushion front*

7 Topstitch the flowers either by hand or with free machining using a slightly contrasting thread. I find the slightly rustic edge in this fusible appliqué very pleasing for these flowers.

Daisy and Lavender Cushion   83

8 Draw in the lavender stems. I do this freehand – imagine them blowing in the wind. Sew the stems with backstitch (see Embroidery Stitches: Backstitch) or couch down the stems with the machine from the back. Leave a long thread end to use for sewing in the little leaves that occur about two-thirds up the stem. Use backstitch for the lavender head, slightly sloping the stitches upwards as shown in Fig 5.

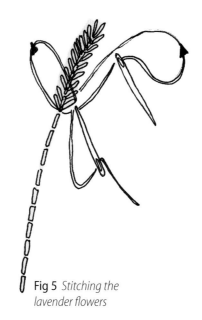

Fig 5 *Stitching the lavender flowers*

9 Once the appliqué is finished, the front should measure 20½in x 24½in (52cm x 62.2cm). Take the piece of backing fabric cut earlier and join it to the cushion front along the top edge.

10 Take Piece M cut earlier and fold in a ¼in (6mm) hem twice along the right-hand side and sew the seam. Lay the cushion front/back out flat and lay Piece M on the right-hand side, as shown in Fig 6. Sew the side piece to the front/back piece.

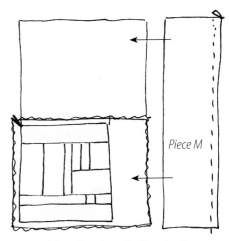

Piece M

Fig 6 *Adding the side to the front/back piece*

11 Fold the cover in half across the width and pin the left-hand side and bottom edges together. Sew together, with the lining stretched out down the one side and across the bottom. Clip corners and turn right way out. Push the lining inside until about 4in (10.2cm) is on the inside. With matching thread machine sew ½in (1.3cm) in from the edge. Press and then hand quilt ½in (1.3cm) in from the seam.

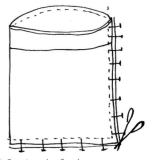

Fig 7 *Sewing the final seams*

12 Lay the cushion cover out flat, right side up, and mark the six buttonholes along the right-hand side on the front of the cover. Do the same on the back, matching up the buttonhole marks (Fig 8).

13 Measure the length of the buttonhole required. Use the bound buttonhole function on your machine if you have one. Cut a piece of fabric to bind each buttonhole – a piece 2in x 3in (5cm x 7.6cm) should be sufficient – and follow the instructions in General Techniques for Bound Buttonholes. Insert the cushion pad when the buttonholes are finished.

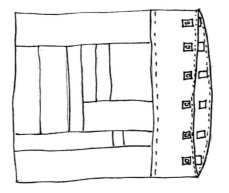

Match up the positions of the buttonholes on the front and back

Fig 8 *Marking and sewing the buttonholes*

tip *Many people don't realise that they have a bound buttonhole function on their sewing machines. It does create a professional finish so it is worth looking in your sewing machine manual.*

14 To make the cushion ties, take the 2½in x 96in (6.3cm x 243.8cm) strip of fabric, fold it in half along the length and sew all around except for a 3in (7.6cm) gap in the middle (Fig 9). Clip the corners and turn out through the gap. Slipstitch the gap closed and then press. Fold the tie in half and starting at the top buttonhole knot the two ends together and then thread it in and out of the buttonholes. When you get to the last hole tie the two ends into a bow.

leave gap

Fig 9 *Sewing the ties*

One Man and His Dog Cushion

Little snippets of farm life creep into all my work, such as the daily tasks of checking the sheep, feeding and bringing them in. Another daily sight is the man and his dog working on the farm – essential characters bonded together in silent watchfulness as they carry on through all weathers. The appliqué scene on this cushion is one seen through centuries of farming – this time with the modern help of the quad bike.

The fields look like patchwork and this is your chance to create your own little landscape. You can also play around with the positions of the appliqué motifs to personalize the design.

Requirements

- Five different green fabrics for fields, fat eighths of each
- Blue and white ticking stripe for sky, fat quarter
- Corn-coloured fabric for corn field, fat eighth
- Floral fabric for meadow, fat eighth
- Brown/green print fabric for hedge, fat eighth
- Scraps of fabrics for farmer's clothes, face and hands
- Scraps of red, black and grey fabric for quad bike, tyres, sheep faces and dog
- Scraps of grey/metallic fabric for feed trough
- Scrap of linen for seed sack
- Scrap of wool for rug
- Boiled wool (or boiled old jumper) for sheep, fat eighth
- Blue denim for cushion border and back, ½yd (0.5m)
- Fusible web ¼yd (0.25m)
- Blending threads for hand appliqué and machine quilting threads to suit fabrics
- Stranded embroidery cotton in brown, white, yellow and grey
- Wadding 25in (63.5cm) square
- Calico 25in (63.5cm) square
- Cushion pad 20in (50.8cm) square

Finished size: 21in x 18in (53.3cm x 45.7cm)

The dog and sheep templates in this project could be used on their own. The two groups of sheep would be easy to enlarge and feature on a pair of cushions. Many of the cushions have patchwork backgrounds you could use for this cushion.

PREPARING FABRICS

1 From the green fabrics cut twenty-one 3½in (8.9cm) squares.
From the blue and white ticking cut one 21½in x 9½in (54.6cm x 24.1cm) rectangle, with the stripes horizontal.
From the hedge fabric cut one strip 2½in x 10in (6.3cm x 25.4cm) and one strip 2¼in x 8in (5.7cm x 20.3cm). For hedge posts cut a strip 8in x 1½in (20.3cm x 3.8cm).
From blue denim cut two strips 21½in x 2in (54.6cm x 5cm) and two strips 24½in x 2in (62.2cm x 5cm) for borders. Cut two pieces each 18½in x 21½in (47cm x 54.6cm) for the cushion back.

MAKING UP

1 To make the main field, take the twenty-one green squares and arrange them into three rows each with seven squares, arranging the squares to form some light and dark areas. Use ¼in (6mm) seams to join the squares together (Fig 1).

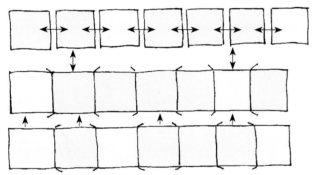

Fig 1 *Piecing the main field*

2 Add the hills and hedge as follows. Place the blue and white ticking rectangle right side up, with stripes horizontal. Lay the corn-coloured fabric over the top to form a hill on the right-hand side. You can judge this by eye or look at the photograph. Turn a hem under the hill, from the top right point down to the bottom left point (by the gate) – this is about 7½in (19cm) in from the right-hand side (Fig 2). Appliqué in place. Now lay on the left-hand side hill (floral meadow fabric) that overlaps the cornfield and appliqué down the top edge. Leave the striped fabric underneath for stability.

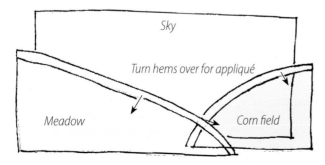

Fig 2 *Appliquéing the hills*

3 Take the 2½in x 10in (6.3cm x 25.4cm) and 2¼in x 8in (5.7cm x 20.3cm) strips of fabric cut for the hedge and fold down the top edge on each strip by ¼in (6mm) (Fig 3). Lay these pieces on top of the meadow and corn field, so that the bottom edges are at the bottom of the sky. Tack (baste) in place (the short ends in the gateway will be covered by the gate posts later).

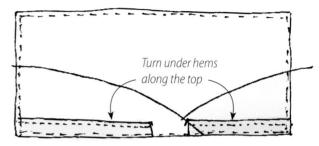

Fig 3 *Adding the hedge*

4 Lay the sky piece face down on the patchwork grass and sew together using a ¼in (6mm) seam. Hand appliqué the top of the hedge, press the sky or top of the block down towards the grass. Take the 8in x 1½in (20.3cm x 3.8cm) strip cut from hedge fabric, fold in ¼in (6mm) along each long side and press. Cut in half, turn up about ¼in (6mm) at each end of the short sides and put each side of the gateway to form posts. Sew around with matching thread.

5 Using a fine pencil, sketch the gate on to the right side of the fabric, positioning it to touch the right-hand gate post. Using brown embroidery thread backstitch on the line. Go over the backstitch with a whipping stitch to make the gate stand out.

Fig 4 *Numbered appliqué parts for the whole design*

6 Begin the appliqué using the templates provided. The various appliqué parts have been numbered on Fig 4. I used needle-turn appliqué for the quad bike, man, dog and feed trough and fusible web for the wool sheep. See the General Techniques: Needle-Turn Appliqué and Fusible Web Appliqué for details. Take the drawing of the quad bike and place it face down on a light box or against a bright window. This will allow you to draw on the back of your patchwork field. Position the bike approximately under the gate, and trace all of the shapes carefully with a fine pencil (Fig 5).

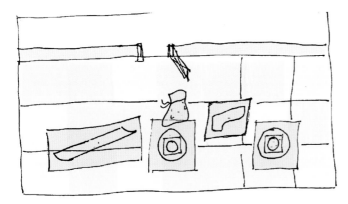

Fig 5 *Starting to position fabrics for the appliqué*

7 Starting with the wheels of the bike (see 1 on Fig 6A), take the grey fabric and place it over the wheel on the right side and tack (baste) around with a contrast thread from the back. Trim to a small ¼in (6mm) seam and sew under. For perfectly circular wheels, use a cardboard template (see General Techniques: Needle-Turning a Circle). Do the same for the inner circles of the wheels (2).

8 Take the red fabric for the bike and lay it on the right side, on top of the patchwork. Pin in place and tack (baste) shapes 3 and 4 from the back. You will only need to sew the top line of the bike and around the back of the dog's feet, as the mud guards will go over the top and finish the bottom edges.

9 Take the black fabric and in the same way tack (baste) on the mudguards (5 and 6), foot plate (7), pillar of the steering wheel (8) and then the handle bars (9). Use a small piece of wool for the rug behind the man (11) (Fig 6B) – I left the lower edge unturned and frayed it instead. Use a small piece of fine denim and tack on the man's jeans (10). Trim and sew down each side of the leg.

Fig 6A *Quad bike appliqué parts*

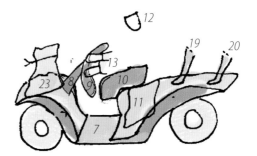

Fig 6B

10 Take some skin-coloured fabric, tack (baste) on the head (12) and hands (13) and sew under. Take the shirt fabric, tack on the farthest arm (14) and sew around (see Fig 4). I left extra to fold up and make a cuff. Tack on the shirt (15). Fold a little piece double for the collar and put under the top of the shirt. Sew around, leaving the collar standing free. The bottom of the shirt will finish the top of the jeans. Tack on the left arm (16), making a cuff, and sew around. Take a little piece of a fabric, tack on the cap (17) and sew under. I used tweed and over-sewed it to prevent fraying, rather than turning under. Using black fabric, add the boot (18).

11 Take a piece of black and tack (baste) on the two off-side legs of the dog (19 and 20) and sew under, leaving enough to go under the dog's body. Tack on the complete body/head/tail of the dog (21) and sew under. Sew a little piece of white for the chest (22) and then embroider or quilt the collar. You could embroider the chest with white stitches if you prefer. Using white embroidery cotton, add some stitches for the tip of the tail and the feet. Using a piece of linen, add the feed sack (23).

12 Draw the feed trough in position and use grey or metallic fabric to appliqué the inner section (24) – see Fig 7. Add the dividing bars (25), the two feet (26), the front of the trough (27) and then the semicircular end of the trough (28).

13 With fusible web, trace on to the patchwork the foreground sheep's bodies (29, 30, 31 and 32). Lay the sheep drawing face down and place the fusible web rough side down and trace onto the smooth side. Place the fusible web onto the back of the wool fabric and iron on firmly, being careful not to scorch the wool. In the same way, trace the sheep faces (33, 34, 35 and 36) and iron onto black fabric.

14 Cut the sheep out with small sharp scissors, make a little score in the back and remove the paper. Place the sheep on the patchwork and iron in place – some of the sheep's legs will go under the feed trough.

15 Repeat this process with the remaining sheep and their faces (37, 38, 39, 40, 41 and 42). Stitch the legs of the four sheep in the far background with dark grey backstitch rather than appliquéing them.

Fig 7 *Foreground sheep appliqué parts*

16 To finish making up the front of the cushion, take the two 21½in x 2in (54.6cm x 5cm) denim strips cut earlier and sew to the top and bottom of the picture using ¼in (6mm) seams. Press seams outwards. Sew the two longer denim strips to the sides, pressing seams outwards.

17 Place the wadding (batting) and calico behind the cushion front. With fine grey/brown sewing cotton embroider the man's face with backstitch and a French knot eye. With white embroidery thread sew some chain stitch daisies over the patchwork field, being careful not to gather up the backing fabric. Use pale yellow embroidery thread to backstitch the sun and its rays. Use green thread to machine quilt some grass in places. Machine quilt the trees and birds in dark grey. Place the work face down on a soft towel and press gently from the back.

18 You can hand quilt and outline all the appliqué, or machine quilt as I did. Stitch the sheep faces in white. I didn't stitch the eyes as I felt they had enough character. If you want to add eyes use a straight stitch or a small irregular cross stitch.

19 For the Oxford-style cushion back use the two 18½in x 21½in (47cm x 54.6cm) pieces of denim cut earlier and follow the instructions in General Techniques: Making an Oxford-Style Cushion Cover. Hand quilt or machine quilt in the ditch between the border and the picture to create a flat edge to the cushion. Insert the cushion pad to finish.

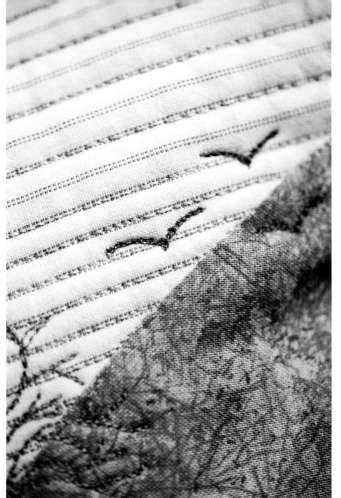

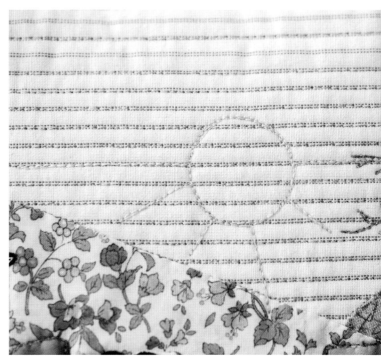

I just love it when you turn this cushion over and see the sheep peeping around the corner. There is always a naughty one that goes the wrong way. Have fun adding your own special touches.

Advent Quilt

Christmas is such a wonderful time and this lovely advent calendar quilt will make the occasion even more memorable. The quilt has twenty-four houses, each with a special little charm hanging behind the three-dimensional door. As you count down the days to Christmas, the charms can be removed from the houses and hung on the appliqué tree. The central house is opened on Christmas day, with the star (or fairy if you prefer) hung on the top of the tree.

This quilt is great fun to stitch. Each house is numbered and they can all be stitched a little differently, so you can have fun customizing them. For a quicker result you could use fusible web appliqué instead of needle-turn, edging the appliqués with blanket stitch or other stitch of your choice.

Requirements

- Background snowflake fabric for bottom of foreground, 28½in x 12½in (72.4cm x 31.7cm)
- Background star fabric for sky, 28½in (72.4cm) square
- Print fabric for inner border, two strips 1½in x 28½in (3.8cm x 72.4cm) and two 1½in x 42½in (3.8cm x 108cm)
- Linen fabric for outer border, two strips 1½in x 30½in (6.3cm x 77.5cm) and two 2½in x 46½in (6.3cm x 118cm)
- Scraps of about twenty-five print fabrics (stripes, plaids, checks) for houses and roofs and snowflake fabric for some roofs
- Fabric for the large house, eaves and roof, two fat quarters
- Print for patchwork bed cover, 6in (15.2cm) square
- Fabric for wallpaper behind bed, 8in (20.3cm) square
- Fabric for the wooden bed, 6in (15.2cm) square
- Pale sheet-like fabric 6in x 4in (15.2cm x 10.2cm)
- Scraps of various Christmas prints for some windows
- Scrap of red felt for heart in large house
- Scraps of fabric for doves, cat, cow, horse, reindeer and dogs

- Boiled wool for sheep's body, fat eighth
- Piece of knitted boiled jumper for reindeer's scarf
- Cream felt for stockings 6in (15.2cm) square
- Scraps of Christmas fabrics for bunting triangles
- Narrow bias strip for hanging bunting 1yd (1m) x ½in (1.3m) starting width
- Green print for Christmas tree, fat quarter
- Christmas fabric for tree pot, 6in (15.2cm) square
- Twenty-four wooden charms and fifty small buttons
- One willow star or fairy for tree top
- Permanent fabric marker with fine tip
- Cotton wadding (batting) 40in x 52in (102cm x 132cm)
- Backing fabric 40in x 52in (102cm x 132cm)
- Perle threads for embroidery in red, black and cream
- Quilting threads in off-white and silver

Finished size: 32½in x 44½in (82.5cm x 113cm) approx

This quilt is perfect for using up some of the buttons and charms you've collected. Try to find different charms for each day of the calendar. Hang the charms around the buttons, twisting them so they don't fall off.

PREPARING FABRICS

1 The 28½in x 12½in (72.4cm x 31.7cm) background fabric for the bottom of the picture foreground needs to be thin enough to see through for tracing if you are using my needle-turn appliqué technique. If you are using a fusible web technique this doesn't matter. The 28½in x 28½in (72.4cm x 72.4cm) pale star or snowflake sky background fabric also needs to be thin enough to see through for tracing.

2 For the narrow inner border cut two strips 1½in x 28½in (3.8cm x 72.4cm) for the top and bottom of the quilt and two strips 1½in x 42½in (3.8cm x 108cm) for the sides of the quilt. For the outer border cut two linen strips 2½in x 30½in (6.3cm x 77.5cm) for the top and bottom of the quilt and two strips 2½in x 46½in (6.3cm x 118cm) for the sides of the quilt.

3 For the Christmas tree make about 2⅛yd (2m) green bias strip by taking the fat quarter of fabric and cutting it into ½in (1.3cm) wide strips diagonally, i.e., along the bias direction. I used a bias maker to create a finished binding ¼in (6mm) wide.

MAKING UP

1 Start by taking your two background pieces and machine together across the 28½in (72.4cm) width. Press the seam downwards. Take the top and bottom inner border strips, sew on with a ¼in (6mm) seam and press outwards. Add the side borders in the same way. Repeat this with the outer border strips.

2 Begin the appliqué, using the template provided. I used needle-turn appliqué – see General Techniques: Needle-Turn Appliqué. Tape the design *face down* on a light box or against a bright window. Place the background fabric *right side down* and trace the complete design on the back (tracing in sections).

If using a fusible web technique to bond the appliqué in position you do not need to trace – just lay your background right side up on the drawing, and prepare all your appliqué pieces as described in General Techniques: Fusible Web Appliqué.

3 Appliqué the big house first, using the fabrics you've chosen. The house is positioned in the centre of the quilt with its base on the lower 'snow' fabric background. The windows, bed and people are worked first, followed by the house itself. Referring to your traced design, pin the fabric for the windows right side up on top of the background, also right way up (see Fig 1). Turn the work over and tack ⅛in–¼in (3mm–6mm) outside all the window lines and around the background of the top of the bed (shown by a green line on Fig 1). You do not need to sew these edges as they will be covered by the house fabric later.

Fig 1 *Tacking (basting) the windows in position*

4 Take the 6in x 4in (15.2cm x 10.2cm) piece of pale sheet-like fabric, fold over ¾in (2cm) twice along the longest side. Slip the bed cover fabric up under the fold, lay both fabric pieces in position and tack (baste) in place (Fig 2). This will give the appearance of a sheet folded over a bed cover. Now tack (baste) on the bed end. Add the two end pillars, followed by the bed knobs (Fig 3). Sew all these bed pieces down in order.

5 For the children in the bed, make a card template the size of the little faces. Gather the fabric around the card with a running stitch, press and remove the template. Repeat for all five faces. Using a permanent fabric marker with fine tip, draw on the facial features and then sew the circles down. When halfway round each face push in a little stuffing to slightly raise the face. You can add different embroidered hair to each character using cream perle thread (see picture).

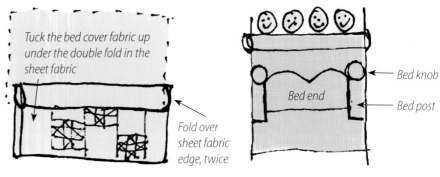

Tuck the bed cover fabric up under the double fold in the sheet fabric

Fold over sheet fabric edge, twice

Fig 2 *Preparing the bed covers*

Bed knob

Bed end

Bed post

Fig 3 *Preparing the bed and children*

6 Pin the main house fabric over the top of the tacked (basted) windows, bed and so on. From the back of the work and with a contrasting coloured thread, tack all the way around on the black solid line of the template (shown as dashed lines in Fig 4), all the windows up under the eaves, down the sides of the house and around the door across the bottom. Turn back to the right side and trim the seam to smallish ¼in (6mm) and then sew under all edges except for the sides of the door. For the windows, cut out a square hole ¼in (6mm) inside the window and then turn the edges under to reveal the picture or window fabric (marked in red in Fig 4).

For a charming decorative look to the main house you could use a ribbon or tape with a festive greeting already printed on, for example, Happy Christmas.

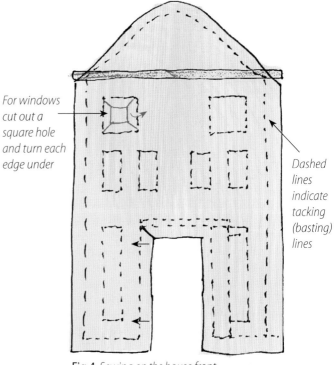

For windows cut out a square hole and turn each edge under

Dashed lines indicate tacking (basting) lines

Fig 4 *Sewing on the house front*

7 Trace the door template and then make two doors as shown in Fig 5. Fold the fabric in half, sew down each raw-edge side and trim the corners. Tuck the doors into place and sew down the side of the door. You can leave the doors with a little gap between or overlap slightly.

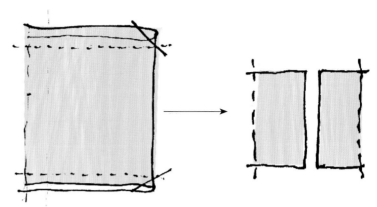

Fig 5 *Sewing the house doors*

Fig 6 *Adding the rest of the house*

8 Sew a piece of ribbon or tape in place as a beam for the doves to sit on. Tack (baste) on the doves and sew down. Now add the porch roof, the heart and the house roof (Fig 6). You could use a white snowflake fabric to resemble snow on the roof.

9 I made a felt stocking for each family member to hang on the bed. Fold the felt piece in half and use the template to mark the shape five times. Cut out and blanket stitch together on the edges, leaving the top open. Stitch the stockings to the bed end with little buttons.

10 Lay a piece of snow fabric for the path and mark the foot prints so when you get to the quilting stage you can quilt them, as if Father Christmas has left his mark!

11 Using the appropriate templates repeat the tacking (basting) and sewing-under process for all of the other houses and three-dimensional doors. You will find it easier to embroider the number on the door *before* you sew the door down. You can number the doors in any order you like. If you have time, make each house a little different, adding extra stitchery, bias strip door posts, buttons, hearts and so on.

 tip

This project is the perfect opportunity to do your own thing – embellish all you like! The gingerbread men on the tree for example are a lovely three-dimensional addition. They are about 1½in (3.8cm) tall and are made by laying a piece of printed fabric on top of wool felt and sewing together by free stitching around the edge. Cut out the shape with small, sharp scissors, being careful not to cut the stitches. Use embroidery thread to backstitch the head, hands and feet details.

12 Now stitch the appliqué for the dog. Fig 7 shows this three-stage process, starting with body (1) then adding the leg (2) and finally the tail and ear (3).

Fig 7 *Appliquéing the dogs*

13 Appliqué the sheep, cow and reindeer in the same way as the dogs, starting with the back legs and then the body. The cow is positioned so the feet are slightly into the border. Make a plaited tail from embroidery threads. For the reindeer, sew on the two legs first. Lay the scarf in position and then sew on the ears and tail and then the body. Add the head last, over the scarf (Fig 8).

Fig 8 *Appliquéing the reindeer*

16 For the Christmas tree use the green bias strip prepared earlier. The top of the tree and star are positioned over the main house. Place your patchwork over the template, pin the trunk in place and sew the edges under. Position the branches and sew them down. Finally, sew on the pot. At this stage gently mark on the patchwork the trees that will need to be embroidered or quilted.

17 Layer up the quilt with wadding (batting) and backing fabric. I machine quilted but use whichever method you prefer. Use silver thread to quilt in the windows, to outline the houses, to quilt some snowflakes and Father Christmas' foot prints. Stitch the trees and chimney smoke in silver by hand or machine. Take care not to melt metallic threads when pressing work. Backstitch the reindeer antlers in brown, with cross stitches for the eyes. Sew on all the buttons, on the tree and behind the house doors, to hang the charms. Hang the charms behind the doors. Add gingerbread men to the base of the tree.

14 Appliqué the cat and horse in the same way, sewing the horse body first and then adding the head.

15 To make the bunting, use the template to cut out little triangles ¼in (6mm) larger than needed, with similar sizes of backing fabric. You could embroider 'Happy Christmas' with your sewing machine if you have one with this facility, or embroider by hand. If using a machine, choose the font and then take pieces of fabric and sew all the letters. Make up the bunting by placing the flag and backing right sides together, sew around two long sides and turn right way out (Fig 9). Take the narrow binding prepared earlier, fold it over the tops of the triangles to join them all together and sew to secure. To keep the bunting hanging free I attached it after I had finished the quilting, trailing it over and under the houses.

Fig 9 *Making the bunting*

18 Bind your quilt, as described in General Techniques: Binding. Make a hanging sleeve, so the quilt can be hung as a decoration – see General Techniques: Making a Hanging Sleeve.

General Techniques

This section contains all the advice you need on the general techniques used in the book. Specific techniques for each project are included in the project instructions.

CUTTING AND PIECING

All the projects in this book have been made using Imperial measurements and although metric conversions have been given in brackets the best results will be obtained using inches. A ¼in patchwork foot on your sewing machine is very useful for sewing accurate seams. A rotary cutter, self-healing mat and quilter's ruler were used to mark and cut out fabrics. Always keep your cutter safe from children and animals and your mat flat and out of the sun.

tip

Check your ¼in patchwork foot as follows. Cut two 2½in (6.3cm) squares, put them right sides together, edges aligned, and sew with the right-hand side of the foot along the edge of the squares. The squares should measure 2¼in once sewn together. If they don't your seam isn't ¼in, so move your needle position so that it is. Put a sticky note on your machine to remind you that you've moved the needle.

Squares and Rectangles

- When cutting shapes such as squares and rectangles, add ½in (1.3cm) before cutting, to allow for a ¼in (6mm) seam all round. Use ¼in (6mm) seams, unless project instructions say otherwise.
- When cutting fabric always put your ruler exactly on the edge of the fabric, so you can just see the edge of the fabric between the dots or line on the ruler.
- Accurate measuring and cutting will also help when joining borders to a quilt so that they fit exactly. When adding a long border you must measure the already sewn components. If you quickly cut a long strip and just add it you will end up with all your borders being different lengths and the quilt looking wobbly.
- Pin shapes together before sewing, unless they are quite small.
- I do not machine stitch forwards and reverse back to start and finish as this makes a lump. The seam ends will be secured when the next seam is sewn over it.
- When sewing long strips together, pin at each end, so the edges are aligned, and then add further pins between. Put the pins in at right angles to the fabric edge, to avoid sewing over pins and breaking the machine needle.
- Cut along the straight grain of the fabric when possible. This direction is the least stretchy, so your piecing will be more stable.
- Sometimes stretch is desirable, particularly when cutting fabric intended to curve, such as binding or fabric for appliquéd stems. Cut the fabric in strips on a 45-degree angle (the bias direction).

- When sewing four squares together to make a four-patch unit, sew two squares together as Fig 1 (right sides together) and press the seam towards the darker fabric. Sew the next two squares together and press the seam in the opposite direction. When the two units are sewn together the seams will fit together neatly.
- When sewing squares or rectangles together in rows, press the seams as shown in Fig 3, so the rows will nest nicely together. When the rows are sewn together press the seams open. If sewing by hand, press the row seams to the side, for strength.

Fig 1 *Joining two squares*

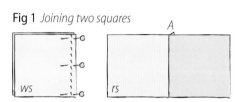

Sew the squares together and press the seam towards the darker fabric

Fig 2 *Making a four-patch unit*

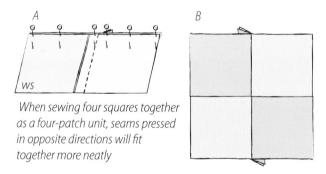

When sewing four squares together as a four-patch unit, seams pressed in opposite directions will fit together more neatly

Fig 3 *Joining squares and rows together*

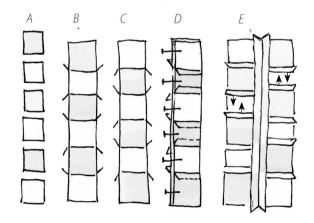

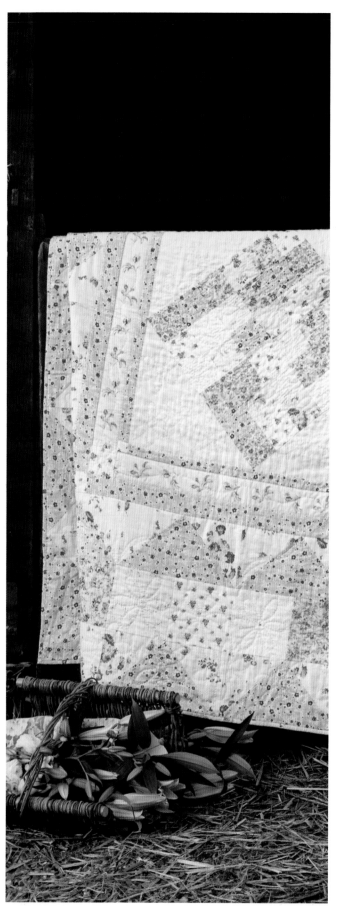

Triangles

- To cut two triangles from a square, decide what size the finished triangle needs to be and add ⅞in (2.2cm) for a seam allowance. Cut a square to this size and then cut the square in half across the diagonal.
- To cut four triangles from a square, work out what size the finished triangle needs to be and add on 1¼in (3.2cm) for a seam allowance. Cut a square to this size. Cut the square in half across the diagonal, and then across the other diagonal.
- When cutting triangles try to have one straight edge of the square parallel with the selvedge so that the long side of the triangle is on the straight grain.

MACHINE SEWING

- For general piecing and sewing, sew with a thread that will blend with the majority of the fabrics you are using. I like to use cotton thread, either Gütermann 50/2, Aurifil 50 or for a specific colour Mettler 50, which is lovely but a little more expensive.
- For a very fine stitch, a 60 weight thread is good and makes a very flat seam, but I don't think it's robust enough for quilts used every day, so I use a 50 weight.
- Choose a stitch length that will form a secure seam but not be so long that the stitches could get caught, break or show, but not so short that the stitches would be difficult to unpick. I use a stitch length of 2.2, which is the default on my machine. If the machine is correctly tensioned the stitches should be invisible.
- Remember to change your machine needle regularly – every eight to ten hours of sewing time, depending on what fabric you are using and what sewing you are doing. Quilting blunts needles more quickly than general piecing.
- When you change threads always cut the thread and pull it out through the needle. Pulling backwards is more likely to lead to a tangle.
- When threading up the machine make sure the presser foot is up and that you insert the thread properly into the tension guide. Bring up your bottom thread with the tension guide up, as once it is down the tension is engaged and you can't move the thread.
- When you finish sewing, sew onto a small piece of fabric or thread saver, as this will stop the needle becoming un-threaded when you start sewing again.
- People sometimes worry about the weight of fabrics to use when piecing but you can mix weights. I avoid heavy linens but as well as using traditional patchwork cottons I also select some light linens and various glazed furnishing fabrics.

PRESSING

- Pressing is very important and can make a real difference to your pieced patchwork.
- By pressing the seams in the same direction towards a shape you can enhance the shape or make it appear to stand out from the background.
- Generally, seams should be pressed towards the darkest fabric, to avoid dark colours showing through light ones.
- When pressing appliqué, always press face down on soft towel folded into four. Press from the back so that any details do not get squashed or marked.

MAKING AN OXFORD-STYLE CUSHION COVER

Several of the cushions use this type of cover, including the Rose Basket Cushion and the One Man and His Dog Cushion. You can bind one edge of the back of the cushion if desired for a decorative look.

1 Take the two pieces of fabric for the back of the cushion. On one piece fold in one long side ¼in (6mm) and then fold again ¾in (2cm) and sew down to secure. On the other piece, fold in a similar hem on one long side, or if you are binding the edge for a decorative look, sew on the binding ¼in (6mm) in from the edge. Fold the binding to the back and either machine or hand sew under.

2 Place the cushion front *right side up* on a table and lay one of the backing pieces (the piece with the binding if using this) right side *down* on the cushion front, with the outer edges aligned and the seam towards the centre (Fig 4A). Place the other backing piece right side down on top, outer edges aligned. Sew all around 1¼in (3.2cm) in from the edge (Fig 4B) (or using the seam allowance specified in the project). I go forwards and backwards over the double seams to make them stronger. Clip corners, turn right way out and press seams.

For a flanged look to the cushion, sew in the seam ditch of the outer border all round by hand or machine, or if there is no border then about an inch or so in from the edge all round.

Fig 4 Making an Oxford-style cushion cover

A

First cushion back piece, right side down with hem or binding towards centre	*Cushion front right side up*

Align edges (left, vertical) · *Align edges* (bottom)

B

	Sew all around
	Second cushion back piece, right side down with hem towards centre

Align edges (right, vertical) · *Align edges* (bottom)

COVERING BUTTONS

Covering buttons to suit the fabrics you are using creates a lovely finishing touch. Self-cover buttons are available that make this easy to do. I prefer plastic buttons because the metal ones can allow the fabric to slip.

1 To cover a button, cut out a circle of fabric that will cover the top of the button and tuck into the back. Run a little gathering stitch around the edge of the circle about ⅛in (3mm) in from the edge.

2 Put the fabric circle over the top of the button, pull the thread to gather in snugly around the button. Push on the back of the button, which has a little hole that fits over the button shank, and snap together firmly.

SEWING A BOUND BUTTONHOLE

A bound buttonhole creates a professional finish to a project and is much stronger, especially on loose-weave fabrics. Most sewing machines have a standard buttonhole facility but check your machine manual to see if your machine has a bound buttonhole facility. Fabric sizes are given with these instructions but use the sizes given in the specific project instructions.

1 Cut a piece of fabric to bind the buttonhole – 2in x 3in (5cm x 7.6cm) should be sufficient. Measure the length of the buttonhole required and mark this on your binding rectangle and cushion fabric (Fig 5A).

2 Lay the binding rectangle and the cushion fabrics right sides together and sew a rectangle ¼in (6mm) wide using a 1.5 stitch length (shown by the dotted line in Fig 5B). On a cutting mat, cut a slit with a buttonhole cutter (or with sharp scissors if you don't have one).

3 Push the binding fabric down through the buttonhole slit and through to the back of the fabric. Fold under the edges of the fabric and slipstitch in place on the back (shown by the dotted line in Fig 5C).

Fig 5 *Stitching a bound buttonhole*

INSERTING A ZIP

A cushion cover can be made with a zip, which makes it easy to remove the cover for laundering. Use a thread colour to match the fabric.

1 With a 1in (2.5cm) seam allowance, machine (or hand) sew both ends of the zip gusset, starting and finishing with backstitches (Fig 6A). Tack (baste) the remaining opening closed.

2 Press the seam open. Diagonally tack the zip in place from the back (Fig 6B).

3 Machine (or hand) sew the zip from the right side of the work, removing the tacking (basting) and opening the zip as required (Fig 6C). Check that the zip opens and remove the tacking holding it in place. The ends of the zip opening can be reinforced with a bar tack if desired.

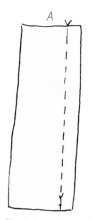
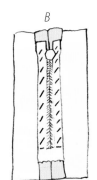
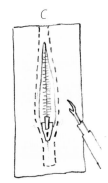

Fig 6 *Inserting a zip*

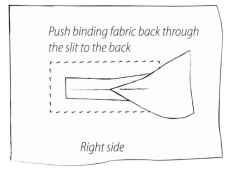

A

Mark buttonhole length required

Right side of cushion fabric

B

Cut the buttonhole slit

Binding fabric rectangle (wrong side)

Cushion fabric (right side)

C

Push binding fabric back through the slit to the back

Right side

APPLIQUÉ

There are two methods of appliqué used in the book – needle-turn appliqué and fusible web appliqué. With needle-turn, the edges of the appliqué are turned under and sewn down; with fusible web a fusible product, such as Bondaweb (also called Vliesofix or Wonder Under) is used to fuse the appliqué fabric to the background.

Needle-Turn Appliqué

I call my version of needle-turn appliqué a template-free method, which is quick, easy and accurate. With this method, the design is drawn on the *back* of the fabric. Cut the background fabric at least 1in (2.5cm) bigger than required, which means any frayed edges can be trimmed later. If a motif is made up of several parts then the farthest parts need to be tacked into place first.

1 Copy the relevant template on to a sheet of paper. Tape the drawing face down on a light box or against a bright window. The design must face down to ensure that the motif will be facing facing the correct way on the front. Place the background fabric right side down, centring it over the drawing, and tape in place. Draw your design onto the back of the fabric with a fine sharp pencil (not too hard) (Fig 7A). Use white chalk on dark fabrics.

2 Remove the fabric from the light box and turn it right side up. Place a piece of relevant appliqué fabric over the shape, positioning it so the straight grain runs from top to tail if the motif is an animal, or if the motif is a curved one, have the grain running with the base fabric (Fig 7B). Pin in place with appliqué pins. Turn to the back and tack (baste) on the drawn line with a contrasting colour thread (Fig 7C). I use a slightly bigger needle, such as a between 8 or 9, and don't knot the thread. Ensure you make a stitch right in the points of the design. Turn back to the front and using small, sharp scissors trim ¼in–⅜in (6mm–10mm) all around (Fig 7D).

3 Using a fine cotton or silk thread to match the appliqué, and a small, fine No. 12 appliqué needle begin turning the fabric edges under by about ⅜in (1cm) and sew down (Fig 7E), removing the tacking ½in–1in (1.3cm–2.5cm) ahead of where you are working. I find it easier to sew around the top of the appliqué from right to left, turning the seam allowance down towards me. If there is a point, fold it flat across the top and secure with two small stitches (Fig 7F). On a pale background you will see a row of pin pricks to help you turn under but you will get used to folding under about ⅜in (1cm). On a sheep's leg or leaf under a rose you only need to sew what's going to be seen, so leave the under-lapped part flat and neat. If there is a tight corner in a design you can clip into the seam allowance slightly, to help turn the fabric under (Fig 7G). Once you have completed appliquéing the whole design place the work face down on the ironing board on a soft towel and press from the back.

Fig 7 *Needle-turn appliqué*

A Draw the design on the back of the background fabric

Wrong side

B Pin the appliqué fabric over the relevant area of the design

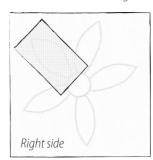

Right side

C On the back, tack (baste) around the shape

Wrong side

D On the right side, trim the appliqué fabric to ¼–⅜in (6mm–10mm) all round

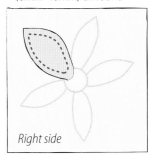

Right side

E Begin to turn under the edges and sew the appliqué in place

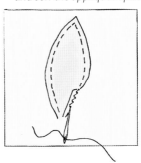

F At corners, fold over the corner for a neat point

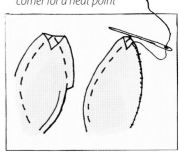

G At tight corners, snip into the seam allowance slightly so the fabric can be turned under more easily

Needle-Turning a Circle

The easiest way to appliqué a circle is to use a card template in the circle size required, gathering the fabric around the circle.

1 Put the template on to the wrong side of the fabric and draw around it. Sew a gathering stitch about ⅛in (3mm) outside the marked circle. Trim the fabric to ¼in (6mm) outside the gathering stitch. Put the template back in place, gather up the running stitch so the fabric folds over the template.

2 Press the circle firmly on both sides to crease the edges and then remove the template. The running stitch won't be seen so can be left in place. The appliqué is ready to be sewn in position.

Fusible Web Appliqué

There are many bonding products on the market. I like Vliesofix Light fusible web as it's a good price and easy to use. The appliqué can be left with a raw edge but it is more usual to edge it with blanket stitch or a decorative machine stitch.

1 Using a light box or window, tape your shape (drawing) face down and trace as accurately as possible on to the back of the fusible web (Fig 8A). Cut out the shape roughly (Fig 8B) – precise cutting is done when the fabric is fused to the web.

2 Place the shape face down on the back or wrong side of the fabric and fuse with a hot iron (Fig 8C). Allow to cool and then cut out the shape accurately with sharp scissors (Fig 8D). Peel off the paper, lay the design in position on the background fabric and iron to fuse (Fig 8E).

tip *Put baking paper (greaseproof paper) on your ironing board and over the shapes to be ironed so you don't get the fusible web on your iron or board.*

3 When the shape is fused in place and cool you can stitch or embellish the edges either with hand running stitch or blanket stitch. You could also machine stitch with straight stitch, zigzag stitch, blanket stitch or other decorative stitch.

4 If you wish to bond a large shape and don't want it to be too stiff, trace the shape and then cut out the central area of fusible web, leaving about ½in (1.3cm) of web around the shape's edge.

Fig 8 *Fusible web appliqué*

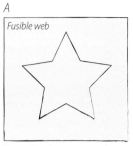

A

Trace the shape on to the smooth, paper side of the fusible web

B

Roughly cut out the shape, leaving about ¼in (6mm) all round

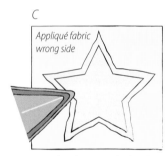

C

Fuse the shape to the back of the appliqué fabric

D

Cut out the shape accurately

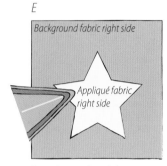

E

Fuse the appliqué shape to the background fabric

tip *If you want a shape to stand out more and have a little more depth, back fabric with fusible web, peel off the paper, fold the fabric in half and fuse to make a fusible web sandwich. Now add web to the back as normal and cut out the shape.*

MAKING A QUILT SANDWICH

There are various ways to layer up a quilt front, wadding (batting) and backing and you may already have your favourite. Some people use pins or safety pins spaced out regularly over the sandwich; others prefer to tack (baste) the layers together in a grid pattern. I like to use a temporary spray adhesive and this is often called spray basting. The important thing is to make sure that all the layers are flat and wrinkle-free. The wadding (batting) and backing need to be at least 2in–4in (5cm–10cm) bigger than the quilt top all round, to allow for reduction in size as the layers are quilted.

Spray Basting

Spray basting with a temporary adhesive is quick and easy (I use the 505 brand). Having someone to help you makes the process even easier. When working with glues, always work in a well-ventilated room and follow the manufacturer's safety advice.

1 Lay the wadding (batting) on the table or floor (covered by an old sheet or paper), shake the can of spray adhesive very vigorously twenty times and then spray the wadding. If the wadding piece is very large I lay the middle on and spray sparingly only what is on the table.

2 Lay the backing fabric right side up on top of the wadding and smooth it out gently, not lifting or pulling. Fold from side to side until all the backing is stuck on.

3 Turn the wadding/backing over and position the middle on the table. Repeat the spraying on the wadding and then lay on the quilt front, right side up, smoothing on gently. At the edges, roll the spare backing on to the front of the quilt and temporarily tack (baste) in place to reduce frayed edges while you are quilting.

tip *If preparing the quilt sandwich isn't your favourite thing, then why not send the quilt off to a long-arm quilter, as I did for the Faded Flower Bed Quilt? Following my suggestions, my friend Sandy quilted wonderful feather patterns, to create a lovely, old-fashioned look.*

QUILTING

Quilting stitches not only hold the patchwork top, wadding and backing together but also create lovely texture and interest over your finished patchwork. The choice is yours whether you hand quilt, machine quilt or send it off to a longarm quilting service. Quilting can be whatever you like – you might prefer to machine quilt straight lines or diagonal grid patterns or to hand quilt motifs that echo the fabrics used. I like to use a mixture of hand and machine quilting. Quilting suggestions have been given throughout the projects and there are many books on the various techniques.

- Begin and end hand quilting with a knot pulled through into the wadding (batting) so it is hidden.
- When machine quilting, I start and finish on the front of the work, stitching on the spot with a 0 stitch length for three or so stitches and then trimming the thread end flush with the quilt.
- Use a suitable thread – there are many hand and machine quilting threads available, so look in your local quilting shop or online.
- Start quilting in the middle of the project and move towards the outside. I use a wooden quilting hoop to keep both sides very flat.
- Try to keep your quilting stitches and the gaps between them even and regular.
- Quilting 'in the ditch', that is, in the seam line, is a good way of securing the layers of a quilt.
- If the quilt is made up of many pieced shapes it can be difficult to quilt accurately in the ditch so you could quilt ¼in (6mm) away from all the seam lines instead.
- If you need to mark a quilting pattern, try the following methods. Masking tape is excellent for marking straight lines. Removable markers are useful for drawing around templates. A blunt-ended tapestry needle is ideal for crease marking shapes.

FINISHING OFF

Once you have finished the quilting, and before you bind and label your quilt, check that it is finished off.

- Lay the quilt out on the table or floor and check you are happy with the amount and distribution of the quilting, adding more if necessary to make sure the layers are well secured.
- With the quilt still flat, measure it to make sure it is symmetrical and that corners are right angled. At this stage I don't trim off any extra fabric from the edge until I have sewn on the binding.
- Thread ends should have been dealt with as you made the quilt but check there are no loose threads.

MAKING A HANGING SLEEVE

Adding a hanging sleeve to your smaller quilts is useful as it gives you the option of displaying them on a wall.

1 Take a piece of fabric 6½in (16.5cm) wide x the width of quilt, plus 1in (2.5cm) at each end. Fold the short ends under to neaten. Fold the fabric in half along the length and machine sew so it resembles a tube. Iron the seam so it is on the back of the tube.

2 Lay the tube on the back of the quilt near the top. Slipstitch in place along both long edges, avoiding stitches showing on the front. Use a length of wooden dowelling to hang the quilt, or perhaps a decorative branch from a hedge.

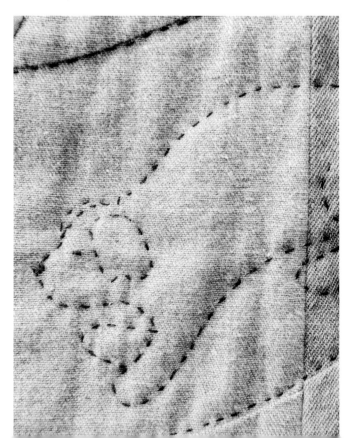

BINDING

People often have a favourite way of finishing or binding a quilt. Sometimes I just turn in the edges on each other but usually I bind them with a single-fold binding. The following instructions are for a double-fold binding but the method is similar for single-fold. I do not trim my quilt edges before adding the binding.

1 Join your binding strips into a continuous length, making sure there is sufficient to go around the quilt plus about 6in (15.2cm) for corners and overlapping ends. With wrong sides together, press the binding in half lengthways. Press the starting end over at 45 degrees (Fig 9A).

2 On the right side of the quilt and starting about 12in (30.5cm) away from a corner, align the edges of the double thickness binding with the edge of the quilt, so that the cut edges are towards the edges of the quilt. Pin to hold in place. Sew with a ¼in (6mm) seam, leaving the first few inches unsewn.

3 At the first corner, stop ¼in (6mm) from the edge of the quilt fabric and backstitch. Fold the binding upwards (Fig 9B) and then downwards (Fig 9C). Stitch from the edge to ¼in (6mm) from the next corner and repeat the turn.

4 Continue all around the quilt working each corner in the same way. Sew over the starting point by about an inch and then trim excess binding.

5 Fold the binding over to the back of the quilt and hand stitch in place with matching thread, folding the binding at each corner to form a neat mitre.

LABELLING YOUR QUILT

When a quilt has been completed it is a lovely finishing touch to label it, even if the information is only your name and the date. Labels can be as ornate as you like, but a very simple and quick method is to write on a piece of calico with a permanent marker pen and then appliqué this to the back of your quilt. You can include whatever information you like, for example, you could say why you made the quilt and who it was for, or for what special occasion, what blocks you used or your inspiration for the quilt.

Fig 9 *Binding*

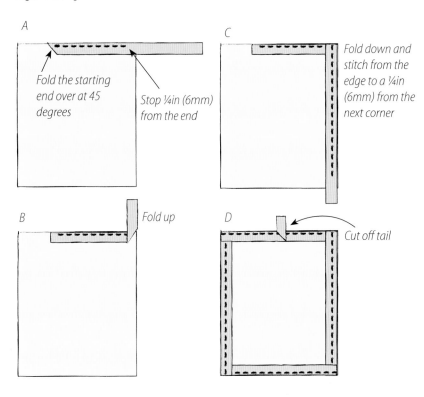

A
Fold the starting end over at 45 degrees
Stop ¼in (6mm) from the end

B
Fold up

C
Fold down and stitch from the edge to a ¼in (6mm) from the next corner

D
Cut off tail

WASHING A QUILT

Some people like to wash their fabrics before they begin a quilt but I only do this when using batiks or very strong plain or patterned colours.

- If you are worried about a fabric then wash before use. If it persists in 'bleeding' even after a cool, short machine wash at 40 degrees, then don't use it.
- The projects in this book can be washed by hand or by machine on a cool or wool setting with a short spin using a non-biological liquid or powder.
- Dry flat on a rack, on top of absorbent towels, preferably in the fresh air or in front of a radiator or Rayburn stove. If dried flat the quilt probably won't need to be ironed.
- When storing quilts, roll the quilt up, right side out. Avoid using polythene bags and keep out of bright sunlight. If stored for long periods regularly change the rolled or folded position to avoid hard-to-remove creases.

EMBROIDERY STITCHES

There are many hand and machine embroidery stitches you could use for patchwork and quilting. The ones used on the projects for this book are described and shown here.

Backstitch

Backstitch is a versatile stitch and can be used to stitch a motif, to add single stitches for emphasis and to outline areas. It can also be 'whipped' with another thread, to strengthen the line or add a second colour.

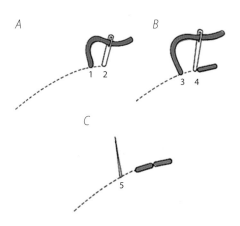

Chain Stitch

This stitch can be worked in straight or curved lines and as a single, detached stitch.

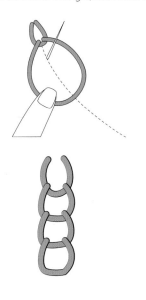

French Knot

These little knots can be used for decorative stitching or focal points such as eyes. Wrap the thread around the needle once or twice, hold the thread firmly and reinsert the needle, pulling the thread through to the back. For bigger knots use a thicker thread.

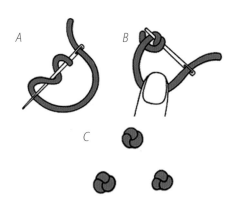

Blanket Stitch

This is the stitch most often used to edge appliqué motifs, especially in fusible web appliqué. When stitched tightly together the stitch can be used for buttonholes.

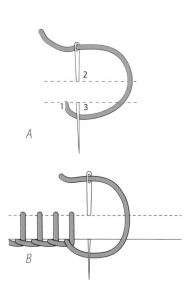

Cross Stitch

This embroidery stitch can be used in many ways – as an edging, a filling or individually as animal eyes.

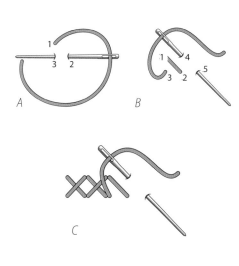

Hemming Stitch

This is worked with fine, small stitches and thread matching the fabric for invisible or blind hemming.

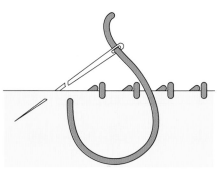

Lazy Daisy Stitch

This stitch is really a detached chain stitch and can be worked in circles for flowers.

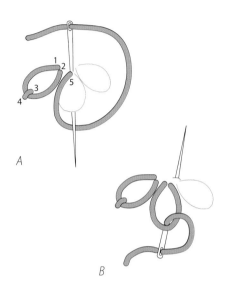

A

B

Topstitch

This is usually done by machine but can be hand worked. It provides additional security on hemmed or folded edges and create a neater, flatter edge. Work the stitches about ⅛in (3mm) from the edge.

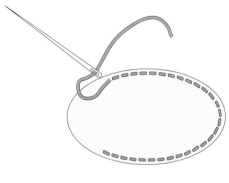

Quilting or Running Stitch

A quilting stitch is really a running stitch and is worked by taking the needle in and out of the fabric at regularly spaced intervals in any direction required.

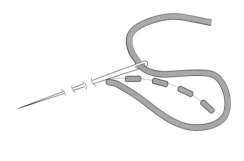

Whipped Stitch

This stitch creates a stronger line than running stitch or quilting alone and can look very decorative if the whipping is done in a different colour, creating a twisted look. Backstitch can also be whipped this way, as can many other stitches.

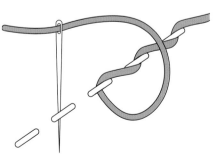

Templates

All the templates you will need for the projects have been supplied in this section, following the book order. Most of the templates have been reduced to fit the page so before using please enlarge them on a photocopier by the percentage given. See General Techniques: Appliqué for instructions on needle-turn appliqué and fusible web appliqué.

Heart Pie Crust Cushion
Appliqué Template
Shown actual size

Vintage Button Cushion
Quilting Templates
Shown actual size

Pie Crust Cushion
Appliqué Templates
Shown actual size

Birds Embroidery Template
Use whipped backstitch

Cow Appliqué Template
Prepare 1

Ear Pattern
Cut 2 from doubled fabric
to make two ears

Heart Appliqué Template
Prepare 1

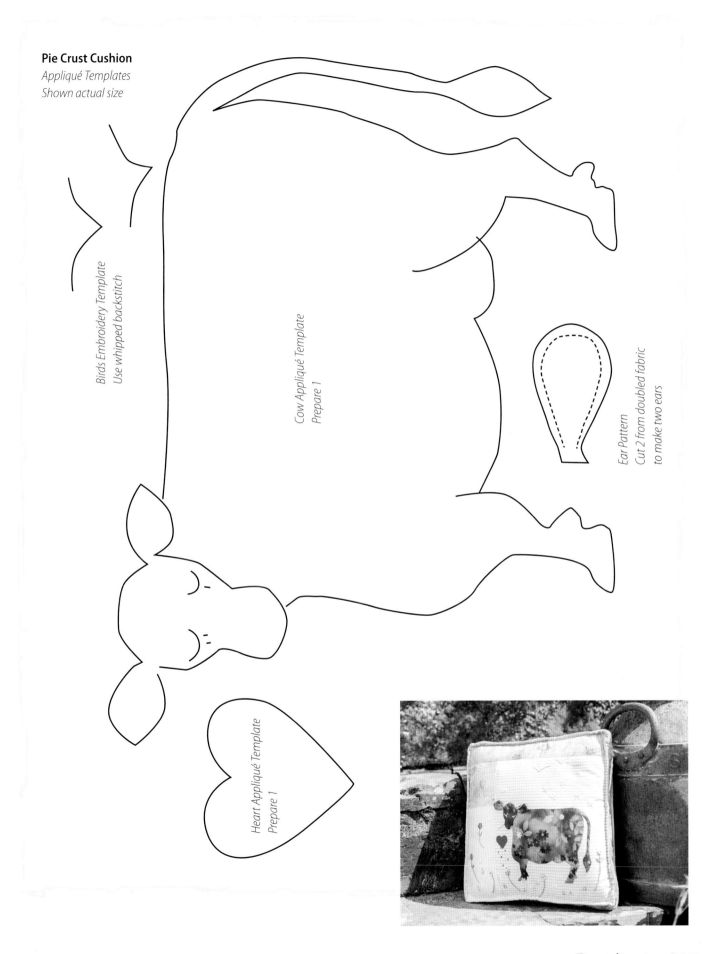

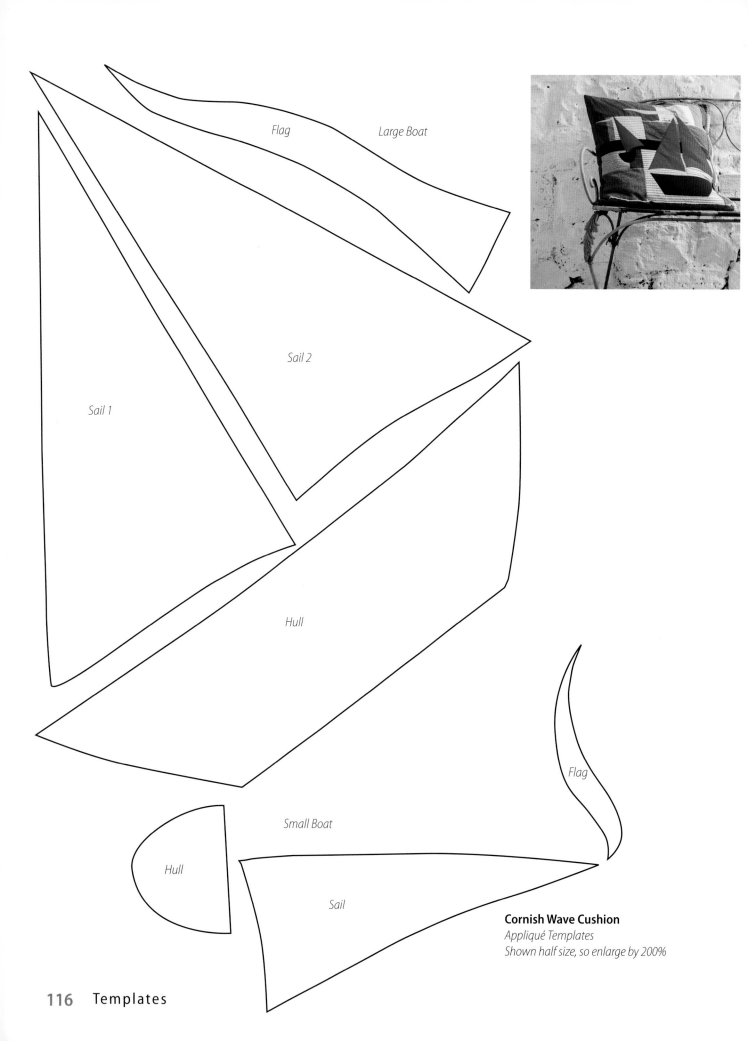

Flag

Large Boat

Sail 2

Sail 1

Hull

Flag

Small Boat

Hull

Sail

Cornish Wave Cushion
Appliqué Templates
Shown half size, so enlarge by 200%

Flower Bed Quilt
Quilting Templates
Shown actual size

Quilt centre daisy

Border daisy

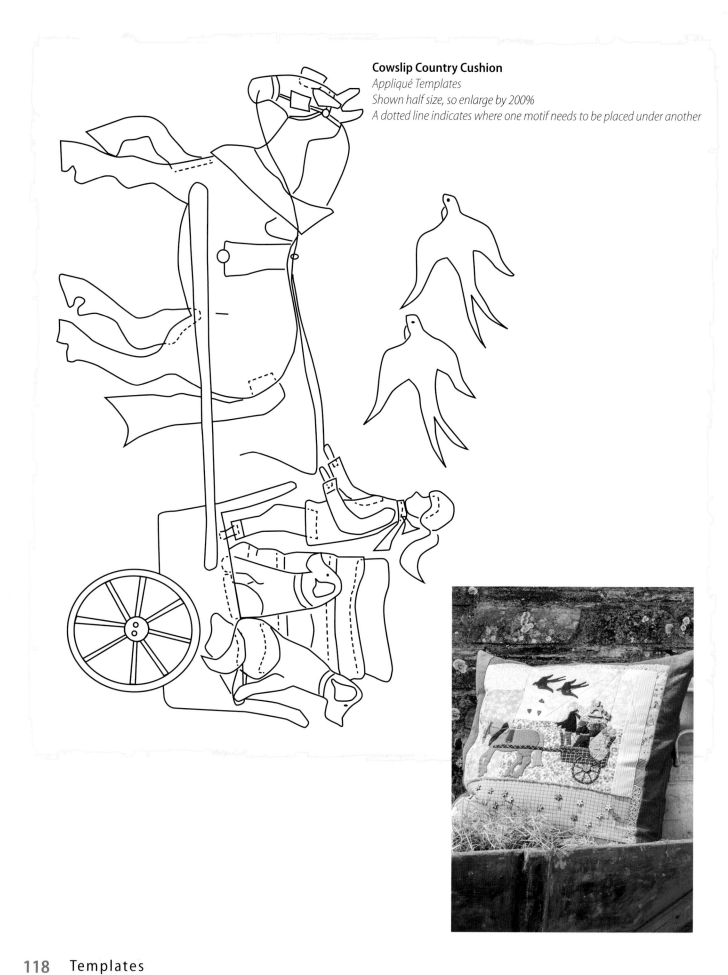

Cowslip Country Cushion
Appliqué Templates
Shown half size, so enlarge by 200%
A dotted line indicates where one motif needs to be placed under another

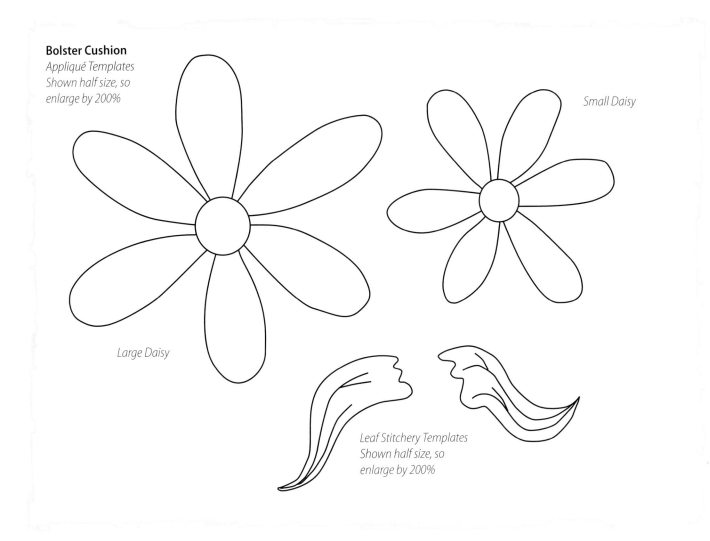

Bolster Cushion
Appliqué Templates
Shown half size, so
enlarge by 200%

Small Daisy

Large Daisy

Leaf Stitchery Templates
Shown half size, so
enlarge by 200%

Individual rose petal templates if required (actual size)

3

Centre

2

8

4

1

9

10

7

5

6

3

8

2

Centre

4

9

1

10

7

5

6

Rose Basket Cushion
Appliqué Templates
Shown actual size
The red lines indicate the basket shape beneath the appliquéd flowers

Embroidered lavender

Leaf 1

2

4

3

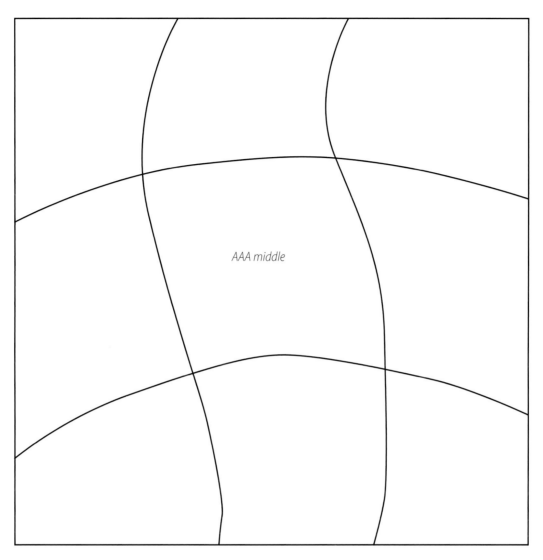

AAA middle

Wobbly Dog Quilt
Block Pattern A
Shown half size, so enlarge by 200%

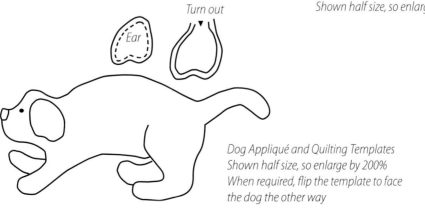

Turn out

Ear

Dog Appliqué and Quilting Templates
Shown half size, so enlarge by 200%
When required, flip the template to face
the dog the other way

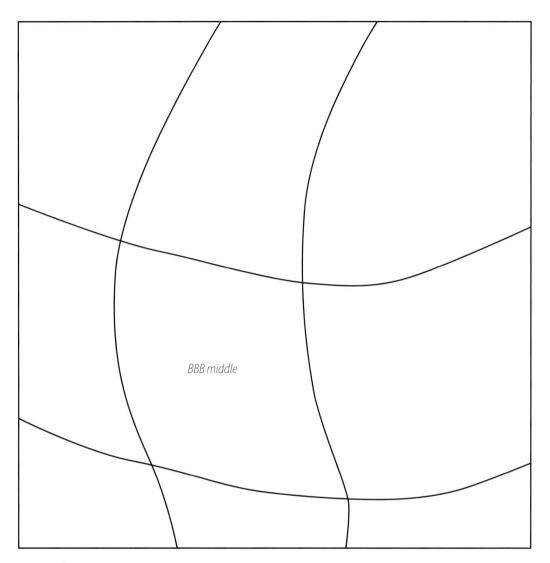

BBB middle

Wobbly Dog Quilt
Block Pattern B
Shown half size, so enlarge by 200%

Daisy and Lavender Cushion

Appliqué Templates
Shown actual size

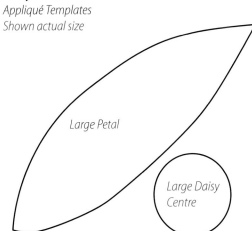

Large Petal

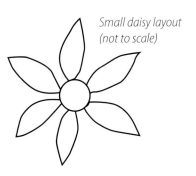

Large Daisy Centre

Large daisy layout
(not to scale)

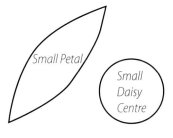

Small Petal

Small Daisy Centre

Small daisy layout
(not to scale)

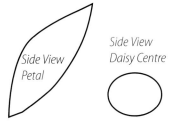

Side View Petal

Side View Daisy Centre

Side view daisy layout
(not to scale)

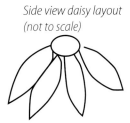

One Man and His Dog Cushion
Appliqué Templates
Shown half size, so enlarge by 200%)

Advent Quilt →
Appliqué Templates
Guide to show the approximate positions of the motifs. Please see pull-out page for actual size

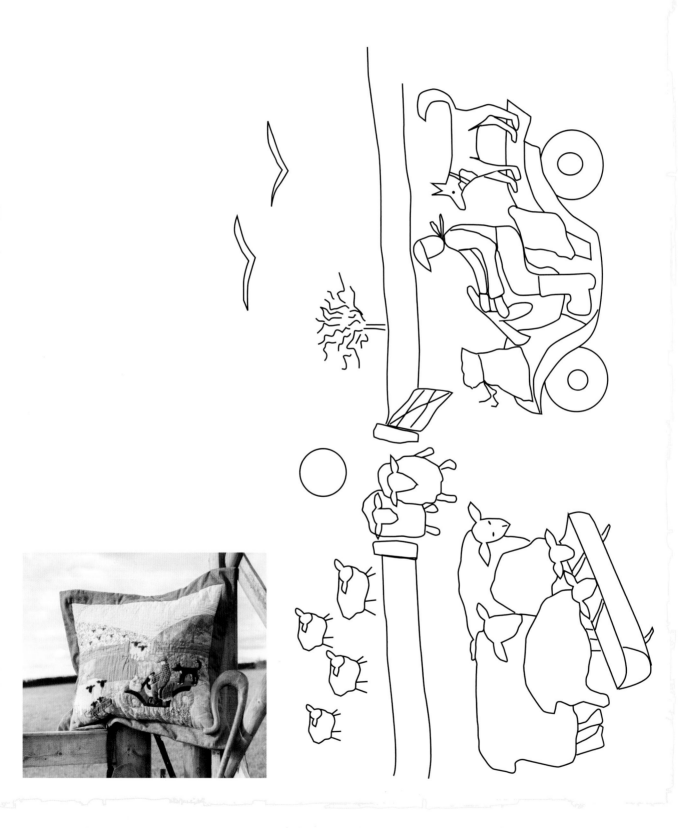

Large House

Doves

Horse

Tree Pot

Cat

Dogs

Reindeer

Sheep

Cow

Suppliers

Bernina (Bogod & Co Ltd)
91 Goswell Rd, London EC1V 7EX, UK
Tel: 02075 497849
For sewing machines

Cowslip Workshops
Newhouse Farm, St Stephens, Launceston,
Cornwall, PL15 8JX, UK
Tel: 01566 772654
www.cowslipworkshops.co.uk
*For fabrics, threads (including hare print and
Gütermann threads), Bernina sewing machines,
classes/workshops and exhibitions*

Donna Flower
Tel: 07896 922694
www.donnaflower.com
For antique, vintage and retro textiles

**Linda Clift Antique Textiles
and Quilts**
Tel: 01305 264914
www.antiquequiltsandtextiles.co.uk
For vintage buttons, quilts and more

Liz Drake Antique Textiles
Tel: 01305 786801
www.oldfashionedstuff.co.uk
For antique and vintage textiles

Lynette Anderson Designs
www.lynetteandersondesigns.com.au
www.lynetteandersondesigns.typepad.com
*For fabric and buttons (used in Cowslip
Country Cushion)*

Moda Fabrics
(main English importer)
Winbourne Fabrics, Unit 3a Brown Lees Road
Industrial Estate, Forge Way, Knypersley,
Stoke-on-Trent, Staffordshire ST8 7DN, UK
Tel: 01782 513380
www.winbournefabrics.co.uk

Sandy Chandler
Kernick Farm, St Stephens, Launceston
Cornwall, PL15 8SW, UK
Tel: 01566 785756
www.thequiltingcompany.co.uk
For long-arm quilting

Stitch Craft Create
www.stitchcraftcreate.co.uk
For fabrics, threads and buttons

Acknowledgments

To write a book is a great honour and something I never dreamed of doing, so thank you to David & Charles for inviting me. English is not my favourite subject – I write as I think and all the ideas just tumble out of my head – so I thank Lin Clements sincerely for tidying me up!

I am truly grateful to David and Annemarie Leather who encouraged and inspired me to a life in fabric and for reassuring me that dreams of running a business can come true. To Daphne and Pepe Turner who sold my first quilts, and to the many other tutors including Nancy Gidley my first teacher, Susan Denton, Deirdre Amsden, Janet Bolton and Charlotte Yde, to name but a few. Through quilting I have met many new friends all around the world who share, sew, talk and are a great support.

I would never have survived all the preparation and work for this book, and continued to run the business and teach without the help of the whole team at Cowslip Workshops, so huge thanks to Becky Stephens, Arnolda Kinvig, Helen Brookham and Jan Whitehouse, who have shared some of the sewing with me. A very special thanks to Sandy Chandler from The Quilting Company, who, luckily, lives just over the hedge! Sandy quilted the blue version of the Flower Garden Quilt and is a marvel at taking your quilting ideas and coming up with just exactly what you want. She also saved the day when I ran out of time making the Advent Quilt. Thanks to the many students who have taken my designs and changed or adapted them with fantastic results. Thanks also to Kath Parsons, who very kindly lent her cow cushion, made in my Cornish Hedge quilt class.

About the Author

Jo Colwill was born and bred in Cornwall and country customs and folklore have had an influence on her work. After some time teaching horse riding, she worked for seven years at Inscape Design, an interior design store, which taught her how to give a house an individual, personal look and how to make something new out of old things. Jo's sister has lived in Norway for twenty-eight years and Jo admires the simple Scandinavian colours and style, and their heritage of weaving, stitching and costume. About twenty-five years ago Jo set up Cowslip Workshops on their tenanted organic farm, which has developed from the kitchen table to a purpose-built workshop, well-stocked fabric store and cafe. She loves teaching the techniques of making a quilt and encouraging students to develop their work in their own original way. Since running Cowslip Jo has met many extremely talented tutors from all around the world. She loves making picture quilts, which capture the colours and customs of the countryside.

Index

A DAVID & CHARLES BOOK
© F&W Media International, Ltd 2013

David & Charles is an imprint of F&W Media International, Ltd
Brunel House, Forde Close, Newton Abbot, TQ12 4PU, UK

F&W Media International, Ltd is a subsidiary of F+W Media, Inc
10151 Carver Road, Suite #200, Blue Ash, OH 45242, USA

Text and Designs © Jo Colwill 2013
Layout and Photography © F&W Media International, Ltd 2013

First published in the UK and USA in 2013

A catalogue record for this book is available from the British Library.

ISBN-13: 978-1-4463-0256-9 UK paperback
ISBN-10: 1-4463-0256-3 UK paperback

ISBN-13: 978-1-4463-0359-7 US paperback
ISBN-10: 1-4463-0359-4 US paperback

Printed in China by RR Donnelley for
F&W Media International, Ltd
Brunel House, Forde Close, Newton Abbot, TQ12 4PU, UK

10 9 8 7 6 5 4 3 2 1

Acquisitions Editor: Sarah Callard
Editor: James Brooks
Project Editor: Lin Clements
Design Manager: Sarah Clark
Photographer: Jack Gorman
Senior Production Controller: Kelly Smith

F+W Media publishes high quality books on a wide range of subjects.
For more great book ideas visit: www.stitchcraftcreate.co.uk